BRITISH RAILWAYS

PAST and PRESENT

No 28

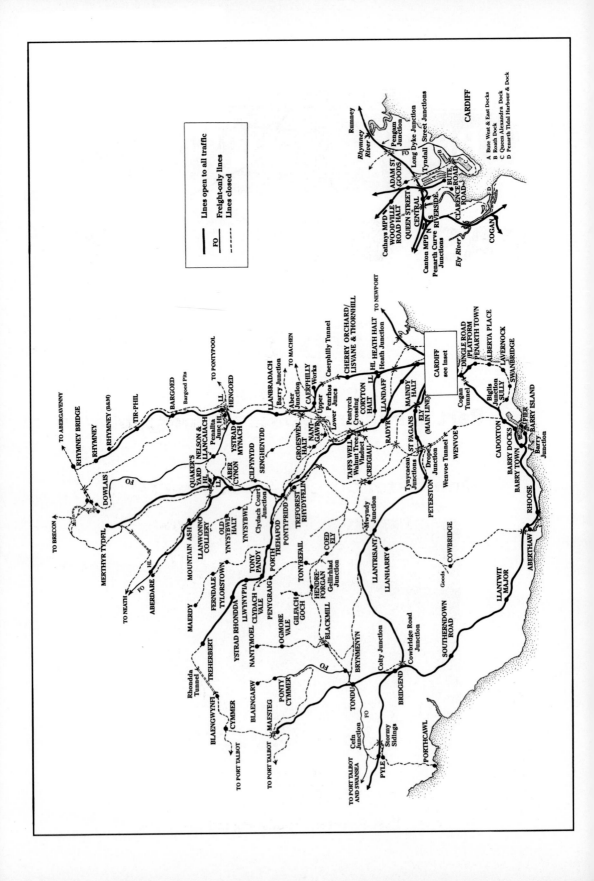

BRITISH RAILWAYS

PAST and PRESENT

No 28

South Wales
Part 2: Mid and South Glamorgan

Don Gatehouse & Geoff Dowling

Past and Present

Past & Present Publishing Ltd

This book is dedicated to the memory of
Jean Dowling (26 November 1941-27 August 1994)
and
Alan Gatehouse (17 July 1942-10 May 1994)

© Don Gatehouse & Geoff Dowling 1995

All rights reserved. No part of this publication may be reproduced, stored in a retrieval system or transmitted, in any form or by any means, electronic, mechanical, photo-copying, recording or otherwise, without prior permission in writing from Past & Present Publishing Ltd.

First published in December 1995

British Library Cataloguing in Publication Data

A catalogue record for this book is available from the British Library

ISBN 1 85895 084 8

Past & Present Publishing Ltd
Unit 5
Home Farm Close
Church Street
Wadenhoe
Peterborough PE8 5TE
Tel/fax (01832) 720440

Printed and bound in Great Britain

Maps drawn by Christina Siviter

CONTENTS

BIBLIOGRAPHY

History of the Great Western Railway, Volumes 1 & 2 by E. T. McDermott and C. R. Clinker (Ian Allan)
Forgotten Railways - South Wales by James Page (David & Charles)
Rails in the Valleys by James Page (David & Charles)
The Barry Railway by D. S. M. Barrie (Oakwood Press)
The Cardiff Railway by E. R. Mountford (Oakwood Press)
The Rhymney Railway by R. W. Kidner (Oakwood Press)
The Taff Vale Railway by D. S. M. Barrie (Oakwood Press)

The Taff Vale Lines to Penarth by E. R. Mountford & N. Sprinks (Oakwood Press)
A Pictorial Record of Great Western Absorbed Engines by J. H. Russell (OPC)
Great Western Engine Sheds, 1947 by E.Lyons (OPC)
Great Western Coaches, 1890-1954 by Michael Harris (David & Charles)
Coal Society by D. Egan (Gomer Press)

PENGAM JUNCTION: Access from the main line to Cardiff Docks is provided via the branch line from Pengam Junction that joined the former TVR Roath Docks branch close to the marshalling yard that had been developed to handle the vast quantities of rail-borne traffic, especially coal. On 30 May 1962 BR Class '9F' No 92220 *Evening Star* was provided to haul the evening Cardiff Docks to Soho Pool tanks. Complete with lined green livery and Great Western-style copper cap to the chimney, this was the last steam locomotive built for British Railways, being delivered from Swindon in March 1960.

The commissioning of the multiple aspect signalling (MAS) in 1966 saw the closure of Pengam Junction signal box and the removal of all semaphore signalling. After the closure of the Bute Docks in the 1970s, activity was centred on the Queen Alexandra and Roath Docks. Cardiff Tidal Yard saw considerable activity through the 1980s with general freight handled by Speedlink services, as well as local metals, coal and petroleum Trainload

activity. Following a major reorganisation in the 1990s, the Allied Steel & Wire Company took over responsibility for operation at Tidal Yard, with British Rail only delivering and collecting traffic. On 18 July 1994 Class 37/0 No 37258 has collected covered steel wagons from Tidal Yard for the short journey to Alexandra Dock Junction, Newport, where the wagons will be incorporated into an RfD service bound for the Continent. *R. O. Tuck/DCG*

INTRODUCTION

It was in 1841 that the Taff Vale Railway Company (TVR) opened its main line throughout from Cardiff to Merthyr Tydfil. This was some nine years prior to the South Wales Railway opening its main line through Cardiff and Bridgend to Swansea. The Second Marquis of Bute had opened a new dock at Cardiff in October 1839 and the new railway was to provide better communication for the ironmasters to transport their products for shipment.

With the production of iron having witnessed rapid growth from the middle of the 18th century, the Merthyr area had developed into the focal point of the iron industry, not only in South Wales but also the world. Prior to the construction of the railway the Glamorgan Canal, completed in 1794, had revolutionised the transportation of finished iron from the isolated forges in the hinterland to the port at Cardiff on the Bristol Channel. However, the canal had soon become the prime means of transport for coal, which by the 1830s had far outstripped iron as the main cargo carried.

As well as the line to Merthyr, the TVR had opened a short branch line to Dinas in the Rhondda Valley, where coal was being mined, and it was the demand for this fossilised fuel that was soon to become more significant in the story of railway development in Glamorganshire than the iron industry around Merthyr. The early mining exploits in the coalfield in East Glamorgan had seen the production of bituminous coal, being suited for domestic, gas and coke manufacture. However, it was the deeper-formed strata that were to become the more sought-after, as it was these steam coals that would be required to fuel the nation's boilers.

The expansion of the coal industry was to see rapid growth in the Rhondda and Aberdare valleys in particular, and by the middle of the 19th century such was the output from the central valleys of the Glamorgan coalfield that the construction of an extension at Cardiff Docks was required. By 1851 the Bute Trustees had placed a contract for the construction of the Bute East Dock and it was these same Trustees who were soon to promote the Rhymney Railway Company. In that same year the Glamorgan coalfield received the ultimate accolade when an Admiralty Report declared South Wales steam coal to be the most suitable for use in the boilers that powered the mighty fleet of the Royal Navy.

The stage was therefore set for a further acceleration both in the number of new pits being sunk, and in the construction of railway lines to serve the growing levels of coal output. As well as the rapid transformation of the once rural landscape into the centre of the nation's coal production, the Rhondda became one of the fastest-growing centres of population in the world. The Llynvi, Garw, Ogwr, Ely, Cynon, Taff and Rhymney valleys also saw a new society develop in the second half of the 19th century that was based on the existence of rich and plentiful supplies of steam coal in the area.

Despite the expansion of the docks at Cardiff, the huge volumes of coal being produced for markets outside the UK identified the need for even more port facilities. In order to relieve congestion at Cardiff, 1865 was to see the Penarth Dock opened by a subsidiary company of the TVR. The railways continued to develop, and towards the end of the 19th century the power and influence of the South Wales steam coal trade was to be no better illustrated than by the growth and prosperity of the Barry Railway. During its separate corporate existence of less than 40 years (1884-1921) the Barry was to established a position that would rank it second only to the Taff Vale Company amongst the independent railways of South Wales. Indeed, the Barry Company was the largest example in the British Isles of a fully integrated dock and railway undertaking to be planned and constructed as such.

The scale of expansion of the South Wales coal industry can be illustrated statistically when you consider that in 1840 less than 5 million tons were mined near the edges of the coalfield.

7

The annual output grew in the next 20 years to over 12 million tons, then in the next two generations to over 24 and 43 million tons respectively. The peak came in 1913, when over 56 million tons were produced, with 37 million tons being shipped through the South Wales ports. Of the total volume of coal and coke exported, over 25 million tons were dealt with by Barry, Cardiff and Penarth docks via the railways that linked them to the collieries.

At the Grouping the GWR was enlarged considerably, in particular by the addition of the various Welsh companies. Of the six Welsh constituents, the Taff Vale, Rhymney, Barry and Cardiff railway companies alone swelled the GWR locomotive stock list by over 560 of the 700 assorted steam engines of all makes and sizes that were brought into the enlarged parent body.

The inter-war years were to see the decline of the South Wales coal industry. Indeed, having once supplied almost one-third of the world's coal exports, by the end of the '20s South Wales only accounted for 3 per cent. Geological difficulties made it more expensive than elsewhere in Britain to mine coal, and oil was a ready replacement in many of its prime uses. Just as coal had been the mainstay of the railway operations during the growth and boom years, it was eventually to prove the weakness. The GWR commenced the process of rationalisation of the intricate railway system that it had inherited, with service cuts and line closures.

Under British Railways' control, the withdrawal of passenger services continued, and in due course line and yard closures were completed when the remaining mineral traffic ceased. The pit closure programme continued unabated even after the nationalisation of the coal industry in 1947, when over 22 millions tons had been produced by a workforce of 108,000. By 1983 production was down to 6.5 million tons and the workforce to 22,000. Before the end of that decade, deep mining had ceased in the Rhondda Fach and Taff Vale, as well as in the western group of Mid-Glamorgan valleys, to be followed in October 1991 by the Rhymney, when Penallta Colliery ceased production.

Apart from the South Wales main line, the core passenger services were now based on the network of lines radiating from Cardiff into the principal valleys of Mid Glamorgan and to Penarth and Barry. Following the sectorisation of British Rail operations, closer co-operation between local BR management and the Mid and South Glamorgan County Councils produced a steady turnaround of fortunes for a system that had previously seen decades of decline.

Better promotion of local rail travel and sound and co-ordinated investment projects saw new stations opened and improved provision of park and ride facilities. By the end of the '80s new passenger services had been introduced in the Cynon Valley to Aberdare and on the City Line to the west of Cardiff. Restoration of passenger services on the former mineral-only line up the Llynvi Valley as far as Maesteg was to follow, and by the end of 1994 the core Cardiff Valleys network was carrying approximately 18-20,000 passengers a day.

Although freight traffic, especially coal, is only a shadow of its former self, the main line sees significant movements of steel and petroleum-based products. The prime users of rail-borne coal are Aberthaw Power Station on the Vale of Glamorgan route and British Steel's production plant at Llanwern.

In order to take you along the railway lines of Mid and South Glamorgan, we will base our coverage on the principal routes of the pre-Grouping constituent companies. Our portfolio of material will provide you with an insight into several decades of railway operations with coverage of key locations as well as the variety of passenger and freight workings that could be seen, both Past and Present.

Sincere thanks are recorded for the photographers who have allowed us to make use of their material. In addition, we acknowledge the assistance provided by the management and staff of the various subsidiary companies of British Rail, especially for permitting access to otherwise restricted locations. Particular thanks are recorded for Alan Jarvis, Bob Tuck and John Hodge, who have provided additional help with information and advice on caption details. Finally, special thanks to Sue Gatehouse, who has supported us throughout this project with great cooking and a dash or two of good humour.

Don Gatehouse
Geoff Dowling

The South Wales Main Line to Cardiff

RUMNEY: On 15 May 1965 ex-GWR '4200' Class 2-8-0 heavy freight tank No 5202 provides a flurry of exhaust as it progresses along the Up Relief line. About to pass on the Up Main line is an Inter-Regional working formed by a BR Swindon-built three-car InterCity unit. Built in 1963, the unit was fitted with the four-character route indicator equipment. The 'M' denotes a destination on the London Midland Region.

Our April 1995 visit to the location recorded Class 56 No 56076 *British Steel Trostre* passing with the thrice-weekly service from Barry Docks to Burn Naze. The train is operated on behalf of European Vinyls Corporation between ICI Hillhouse (Fleetwood) and its Polyvinyl Chloride (PVC) manufacturing plant in Barry Docks. The tank wagons are hired from Nacco (UK) Ltd, and with a single locomotive the train diagram completes three round trips each week. *Hugh Ballantyne/DCG*

RUMNEY RIVER BRIDGE (1): On Sunday 19 May 1957 ex-GWR 'Castle' Class 4-6-0 No 5025 *Chirk Castle* catches the evening sun as it heads east with the 4.00 pm Whitland to Kensington milk train; Swindon-based 'Castles' were the regular motive power for this daily working. A crew change has been made at Cardiff Canton just prior to 7 pm and the driver and fireman will work the train through to Swindon. Beyond the mineral wagons in the storage sidings can be seen the East Moors Steel Works, also known as Dowlais Works.

The East Moors Works had been opened by the Dowlais Iron Company in 1891 and was a prominent feature of the skyline to the east of Cardiff until it was closed in April 1978 and demolished soon afterwards. An elevated section of roadway dominates the background of our April 1995 view with power car No 43165 heading the 1732 Swansea to London Paddington. *R. O. Tuck/GPD*

RUMNEY RIVER BRIDGE (2): The 'Red Dragon' was one of four 'titled' trains to be operated between South Wales and London. On 20 August 1960 an immaculate Cardiff Canton (86C)-based locomotive, No 4080 *Powderham Castle*, at the head of a train of BR Mark I coaching stock in chocolate-and-cream livery, gathers speed following a stop at Cardiff. On the left Pannier tank No 8470 stands near the stop board on the Up Relief line with a local coal working, waiting to set back into Pengam Junction sidings.

In comparison, the corresponding view of March 1995 is somewhat devoid of prominent features. The land once occupied by sidings has returned to nature and Roath Power Station no longer dominates the skyline. A Swansea to London Paddington HST service heads towards Newport. *R. O. Tuck/DCG*

11

PENGAM YARD was the focal point of numerous through services as well as local freight workings in the Cardiff area. On 21 August 1964 '4200' Class 2-8-0 No 4285 draws its train of iron ore hoppers away from the reception line adjacent to the yard, on the final leg of the journey to East Moors Steel Works.

Within three years of the above view being recorded, the 10-acre site had been transformed to provide South Wales with its first Freightliner Terminal, which was opened in June 1967. On Friday 21 April 1995 Class 47/0 No 47210 has been rostered to provide the motive power for the evening Railfreight Distribution (RfD) Freightliner service to Crewe. The train will convey containers for delivery to terminals in the North West of England as well as Scotland. *R. O. Tuck/GPD*

PENGAM JUNCTION: On 30 May 1962 ex-LMSR Class '8F' 2-8-0 No 48450 crosses from the Up Main to the Relief line with a lengthy train of assorted vans. On the left ex-GWR '2800' Class 2-8-0 No 3860 shunts wagons in the 'Back of the Box' Yard. These LMSR Stanier-designed heavy freight engines were first introduced in 1935 and a total of 852 locomotives were built over the next ten years, many of which were for War Department stock. The locomotive illustrated was one of the batch built at Swindon in 1945 that were initially loaned to the GWR, but handed over to the LMSR in 1946/7. In 1956 a number of the Swindon-built '8Fs' were transferred back to the Western Region, and they were easily distinguishable by the modified ejector pipe visible on the left-hand side of the boiler.

The BR Type 4, later Class 47, mixed traffic locomotives were similarly a design built in large numbers, with a total of 512 constructed following their introduction in 1962. With so large a Class, the passage of time has seen a great many variations within the fleet, and No 47145 *Merddin Emrys* carries a customised 'rail blue' livery applied by Tinsley Depot. On 18 July 1994 empty covered steel vans are returned from the Cardiff Isis Link depot to Alexandra Dock Junction Yard near Newport. *R. O. Tuck/DCG*

15

PENGAM, NEWPORT ROAD YARD had numerous rail-served warehouses and was the site of the main domestic coal yard in Cardiff. In a view looking a little to the right of the previous one, '9400' Class 0-6-0PT No 3408 shunts the Yard as part of its rostered duties on 8 April 1958. The locomotive carries a white disc denoting 'target' Y5, being a duty based on Radyr shed. Above the locomotive in the background is the Cardiff Trolleybus Depot.

Single-car Class 153 unit No 153 312 provides an appropriate subject on the short section of the Up Main line visible in our April 1994 view of the location. The former railway land has been redeveloped and a retail complex now occupies the site. *John Hodge/DCG*

CARDIFF, NEWTOWN GOODS: The extensive goods handling facilities that once occupied land to the north of the main line on the final approach to Cardiff are well illustrated in this view taken on 7 August 1965. The 8.40 am service from Pembroke Dock to Derby has had a change of motive power at Cardiff and BR Type 4 'Peak' No D28 (later to become 45 124) has taken over this inter-regional working for the run to the East Midlands.

When the location was visited on 16 September 1993, the redevelopment of the site of the former goods depot was well advanced. Class 47/8 No 47841 *The Institute of Mechanical Engineers* heads the 0748 Swansea to York InterCity Cross-Country service away from Cardiff. This service was the last remaining locomotive-hauled InterCity diagram to operate to and from South Wales and was eventually replaced by an HST formation in 1994. *R. O. Tuck/DCG*

CARDIFF, WINDSOR ROAD STABLING POINT: Long Dyke Junction provided access from the main line to the East Dock area, and at Tyndall Street there was a long footbridge that enabled pedestrians to cross the GWR docks branch. The footbridge also provided a vantage point to view the locomotive stabling sidings, which saw particular activity during the period when Cardiff Canton MPD was being converted to a diesel depot and its former steam allocation had been transferred to East Dock MPD. The nearest locomotive in our view of 10 July 1965 is No 7029 *Clun Castle* (now preserved), which would have worked to Cardiff on an early morning service from Gloucester. The main line passed behind the goods wagons stabled on the left, and on the extreme left of the photograph was the embankment and bridge abutments of the former Rhymney Railway docks branch.

The scene in May 1993 shows the land adjacent to the South Wales main line occupied by a newly opened building supplies firm. The tracks from Long Dyke Junction that are still in situ provide access to and from the sidings that serve the Castle Works of Allied Steel & Wire. *R. O. Tuck/DCG*

CARDIFF EAST DOCK BRANCH was opened by the Rhymney Railway (RR) in December 1857 and Tyndall Street Junction was situated immediately south of the bridge that crossed the GWR main line. The junction provided access to both the Bute East Dock and, in due course, Roath Dock via Stonefield Junction and the running lines of the Cardiff Railway. On 21 March 1957 ex-RR 0-6-2 tank No 36 has just left the docks with the daily 'target' D7 trip working to Bargoed Pits. In the background the dockside warehouses, stores and cranes that served Bute East Dock can be seen. The Dock had opened in 1855 and, following the completion of extensions in 1858/9, provided 46 acres of deep water and 17 coal hoists.

The line from Adam Street Goods to Stonefield Junction closed in January 1965 and the Bute Docks were closed to shipping just five years later. The disused railway embankment remained in situ for many years before being cleared in preparation for the redevelopment of the land, as our April 1995 illustration confirms. With the railway infrastructure cleared and the coal hoists dismantled, work co-ordinated by the Cardiff Bay Development Corporation has seen millions of pounds invested to rejuvenate the former docks area. *R. O. Tuck/GPD*

Cardiff Railway

CORYTON: The Cardiff Railway was very much a late entrant into the arena of railway construction in South Wales. Its attempt to open a line from Treforest, south of Pontypridd, to Heath Junction on the Rhymney Railway was to ultimately end in failure; the Taff Vale Railway (TVR) was successful in preventing the junction at Treforest from ever being used for revenue-earning traffic. The line between Heath Junction and Rhydyfelin was opened for goods traffic on 15 May 1909 and for passenger services from March 1911. However, it was only the southern section of the line that was to prosper, and in July 1931 the line closed north of Coryton Halt. Our view of 2 May 1951 shows ex-TVR locomotive No 346 arriving from Cardiff. A run-round loop was retained until October 1964, by which time DMUs operated all of the branch-line services.

The advance of nature is all too evident when you compare the earlier view with that of 15 April 1995. Class 150/2 'Sprinter' unit No 150 276 is about to depart from the terminus with the 1630 service to Radyr, via Cardiff Central and the City Line. *R. C. Riley/GPD*

HEATH HALT LOW LEVEL: A gap of 41 years separates this pair of illustrations. In 1954 an early evening auto-train from Coryton pauses at the Halt while the driver waits for the starter signal to clear before ex-GWR '4575' Class 2-6-2T No 4580 of Cathays MPD can propel its train towards Heath Junction and off the branch.

The future viability of the Coryton branch was in doubt during the early 1960s and passenger services were severely rationalised in 1962. A year later the line was recommended for complete closure, but strong opposition from the residents of north Cardiff saved the day and the withdrawal of passenger services planned for June 1964 was not approved. Under the Cardiff MAS scheme of 1966 the branch was singled, apart from the double-line section retained at Heath Junction. With the former up line removed, only the down platform remains in use, and in May 1969 the word Halt was dropped from the title. Our 1995 view shows Class 143 'Pacer' unit No 143 612 with a Coryton to Radyr working. *Rev R. W. A. Jones/D. E. Moon*

HEATH JUNCTION: Traffic levels in the early 1950s had declined to the extent that auto-sets provided sufficient accommodation for most of the Coryton branch services. However, four-coach and even five-coach trains could still be seen on the branch, particularly for football and rugby additionals on Saturdays. On 9 July 1953 an assorted rake of suburban stock hauled by an unidentified ex-TVR 0-6-2T was photographed coming off the branch at Heath Junction. Above the second coach is the timber-built signal box, which stayed in use until work was completed in November 1984 that saw the original junction close and a new junction installed several hundred yards further north.

The former railway land released following the opening of the new junction was soon re-developed and our view of the same location on 30 May 1994 shows the total transformation that has taken place. Penarth-bound 'Sprinter' unit No 150 274 passes on the former RR main line. *A. Jarvis/DCG*

Rhymney Railway

HEATH JUNCTION (2): The Rhymney Railway opened the Cardiff Direct Line on 1 April 1871 from Caerphilly North Junction on the original main line to a new station on a site to the north side of the TVR's Cardiff Queen Street station. The line was double throughout when built and the original RR Adam Street station, which was situated on the East Docks Branch, was henceforth used for goods traffic only. Viewed looking south towards Cardiff on 9 July 1953, a brace of immaculate ex-GWR 'Castle' Class locomotives, with No 5006 *Tregenna Castle* leading, head north with the stock of the Royal Train, which was being used in connection with the Queen's post-Coronation tour of the UK.

Although the advance of vegetation has left little to provide a point of reference, the retaining wall on the right is just visible and a roof-top chimney can be seen above passing 'Sprinter' unit No 150 268 in our view of the location taken on 30 May 1994. *A. Jarvis/DCG*

CHERRY ORCHARD SIDINGS were adjacent to the RR line just to the south of Caerphilly Tunnel, and our view of 6 March 1957 looking south shows a train of vans departing for Cardiff, while Prairie tank No 4163 passes with the 1.22 pm Barry Town to Rhymney service. Although the GWR had continued to use 0-6-2T locomotives as the staple motive power in the Valleys for many years after the Grouping, the 1940s had seen numerous 2-6-2T locomotives drafted in from other Divisions. In 1955 a number of the Prairie tanks were allocated to Rhymney shed, and they were a common sight on Cardiff Valleys workings until the introduction of diesel multiple units (DMUs).

In November 1985 a new station, Lisvane & Thornhill, was opened on the site. The project was jointly financed by British Rail and South Glamorgan County Council, and provided 'park and ride' facilities. In August 1995 unit No 150 280 was recorded while working the 1510 Rhymney to Penarth service. The former railway workshops were still in use, although now in the ownership of British Gas. *R. O. Tuck/DCG*

CAERPHILLY WORKS (1): Caerphilly Tunnel, 1 mile 173 yards in length, takes the railway beneath Cefn On and into the Rhymney Valley. Upon leaving the northern portal of the tunnel, the railway turns due west, and on the approach to Caerphilly was once flanked by several private sidings to the south and the RR's main locomotive works to the north. On 7 December 1964 ex-GWR '9400' Class 0-6-0PT No 9488 was photographed shunting in the sidings adjacent to the former Caerphilly Works. In the background are several of the wagons adapted for use on maintenance work in the nearby tunnel.

Although all of the sidings have long since gone, the Works buildings are still in commercial use. On 21 April 1995 'Sprinter' unit No 150 277 approaches the tunnel with the 1125 Caerphilly to Cardiff Bay service. *R. L. Masterman/GPD*

CAERPHILLY WORKS (2): The Rhymney Railway constructed its main locomotive, carriage and wagon works on a 17-acre site in the angle between the main line to Cardiff and the Machen branch. The Works opened in 1902, and although no locomotives were ever constructed there, heavy repairs were undertaken as well as a certain amount of carriage and wagon construction. The GWR undertook further expansion of the facilities in 1926 and 1939 to establish Caerphilly as the principal locomotive and carriage repair shops in South Wales. Our view of the Works taken on 12 May 1956, when the site was visited by a Gloucester Railway Society Tour, shows the extent of the main erecting shop.

With the introduction of diesel motive power in the late 1950s, British Railways no longer had a need for the Works and it was eventually closed in 1963. The main premises have survived in commercial use and our view taken in April 1995 also illustrates the collection of motive power and rolling-stock that has been gathered on part of the site by the Caerphilly Railway Society. *W. Potter/B. Cole*

27

CAERPHILLY was the largest station on the RR system. Originally built as a two-platform station, it was extended in 1913 to provide four through platform roads and a bay at the east end, used by certain trains to Cardiff as well as Machen. On Monday 8 June 1964 heavy freight tank No 5210 trundles through platform 4 with a train of coal bound for Newport. Alongside, within the consist of the northbound freight, are tar tanks *en route* from the Tar Distillation Plant at Caerphilly to Aber Junction Yard.

With the closures and rationalisation of the 1960s, only the passenger services to and from Cardiff survived and the facilities provided by platforms 1 and 2 were sufficient for operational requirements. The platforms on the north side of the station were therefore closed and in due course the site was redeveloped to provide a bus interchange. *R. L. Masterman/DCG*

ABER JUNCTION YARD: The original RR line had opened for goods traffic on 25 February 1858 and for passengers a month later. Sorting sidings were established at Aber and it was here that coal trains from the numerous collieries of the Rhymney Valley area were marshalled prior to onward movement. Viewed from a passing train on 20 May 1965, ex-GWR 0-6-2T No 6654 is about to set off up the Rhymney Valley with a short engineering train. Of particular interest is the ex-Cambrian Railway clerestory coach in the train.

When visited 30 years later the site of the former sidings had been covered by the development of the Trecenydd Industrial Estate, with several of the commercial units visible in our earlier illustration still in use. The south side of the Yard has been cleared of all trackwork and a housing development has covered the trackbed to the west of the site. *R. L. Masterman/GPD*

SENGHENYDD: The Aber branch was opened by the RR on 1 February 1894 to serve the colliery developments in the valley. It extended for just under 4 miles from Aber Junction, and had an almost continuous climb at 1 in 58, with a final section at 1 in 49. The branch was single track, with an intermediate passing place at Abertridwr. During the early 1950s an approximately hourly frequency of service was operated to and from Caerphilly on weekdays only, and an auto-train, typical of this period, is seen here at Senghenydd station. Universal Colliery is visible behind the station.

In 1958 DMUs were introduced on the branch services and the 1961 passenger timetable confirmed that some workings ran through to Cardiff and Barry Island. Withdrawal of passenger services came on 15 June 1964, although the branch continued in use until in September 1977 output from Windsor Colliery near Abertridwr ceased as the mine had been linked underground with the Nantgarw Colliery just over 2 miles away. Visited in April 1995, the former station site at Senghenydd had been covered by a housing development. *Rev R. W. A. Jones/GPD*

PENRHOS UPPER JUNCTION (1): Before progressing up the Rhymney Valley, we will take a brief detour along the original route of the Rhymney Railway into Cardiff. Opened in 1858, the RR line headed west from Aber and descended a 1 in 47 gradient to join the TVR at Walnut Tree Junction (Taffs Well). On Friday 12 March 1965 '5600' Class 0-6-2T No 5613 has reached the top of Penrhos Bank with a train of mineral wagons. The train has been banked up the 'Big Hill' from Walnut Tree Junction by Pannier tank No 9667, and the plume of exhaust just visible above the third wagon provides evidence that the banker is still hard at work on the incline. Both locomotives were approaching the end of their working lives, with 5613 being withdrawn in May 1965 and 9667 only surviving until June.

The line between Walnut Tree and Penrhos Upper Junctions continued in use as a freight-only route until closure in 1982. As each year passes, the trees and undergrowth continue their seasonal advance that will in due course return the majority of the former trackbed to nature. *R. L. Masterman/GPD*

PENRHOS UPPER JUNCTION (2): On 12 May 1952 '5600' Class 0-6-2T No 5653 approaches Penrhos Upper Junction with a train of empty coal wagons being returned to the Rhymney Valley. The locomotive is about to pass between the abandoned piers of the former Barry Railway Extension line, which had opened in 1905 to provide that company with direct access to the Rhymney Valley. The line only survived until 1926, when with the decline in post-war coal traffic the GWR took powers to abandon the Extension Line between Penrhos Lower and Barry Junctions, the latter being on the former Brecon & Merthyr Railway line on the east side of the Rhymney Valley. In the right foreground are the tracks of the former Barry route down to Walnut Tree Viaduct via Penrhos Lower Junction, and behind the locomotive are the lines of the former Pontypridd, Caerphilly & Newport Railway.

Despite being abandoned nearly 70 years ago, the piers of the former Barry Railway viaduct have survived intact and well beyond the closure of each of the three former railway routes beneath them. *R. C. Riley/DCG*

WALNUT TREE JUNCTION was where the former RR line joined the TVR immediately south of Taffs Well station. On 16 April 1957 '5700' Class 0-6-0PT No 8789 drifts down the final section of the 1 in 47 descent from Penrhos Upper Junction with a load of coal from the Rhymney Valley. The 'target' C18 identifies the working as a Cathays duty, and the coal will be taken down the Taff Vale to Radyr Yard. Note the sidings on the right that served a small ironworks sited to the east of the junction.

The 'Big Hill' continued to be used well into the diesel era and pairs of Class 37 locomotives would certainly stir the air above Nantgarw as they flogged up the incline to Penrhos with empty coal hoppers *en route* to collieries in the Rhymney Valley and beyond. The end came in June 1982, when the line was abandoned. A section of the former trackbed above Nantgarw has been incorporated into the Taff Trail, and at Taffs Well a car park has been provided for rail passengers, as our May 1994 visit confirmed. *John Hodge/DCG*

LLANBRADACH (1): Returning to the Rhymney Valley, we reach Llanbradach. Our view looking north from the station footbridge on 6 July 1958 shows ex-LNWR 0-8-0 No 49064 approaching with 'Duty 56' *en route* to Barry Island. Summer Sundays and Bank Holidays would produce numerous excursions from the Valleys to the coast and this particular train would have worked down the Sirhowy Valley from Nantybwch. Joining the Pontypool to Neath line at Bird-in-the-Hand Junction, the train would have continued west to Hengoed, where it would swing south and join the Rhymney Valley line. As a point of detail, one of the station posters is advertising a return fare to Cardiff of 1s 10d.

Also heading for Barry Island, albeit by a different route, 'Pacer' unit No 143 623 catches the morning sun in our 2 April 1994 view of the location. In the background, buildings of the former Llanbradach Colliery are still visible. The colliery raised its first coal in 1894 and at its peak employed over 3,000 men. Coal production ceased in 1961. *R. O. Tuck/GPD*

LLANBRADACH (2): Looking south towards Llanbradach station on 18 May 1957 we see ex-RR Class 'R' 0-6-2T No 36 in splendid form as it heads up the valley with the 'D7' trip from Cardiff Docks to Bargoed Pits. Designed by C. T. Hurry Riches for handling heavy mineral trains, the locomotive was built by Hudswell Clarke in 1921. Unlike others in the Class, which were rebuilt by the GWR with taper boilers, No 36 retained its parallel boiler. After working the Bargoed trip on Tuesday 1 October 1957, No 36 was withdrawn; with sister locomotive No 38, stopped later in that week, they were the last pre-Grouping engines on main-line duties to be withdrawn in South Wales.

On 2 April 1994 'Pacer' unit No 143 615 continues its journey towards Bargoed with the 0805 Valley Lines service from Barry Island. These two-car railbus units were constructed jointly by coach-builders Walter Alexander of Falkirk and the railway engineering firm of Andrew Barclay & Sons of Kilmarnock during 1985-6.

The aluminium, wide-bodied railbuses were designed for local and secondary provincial services, and while the original units were fitted with Leyland engines, the 14 revamped versions used by the Cardiff Valleys Train Operating Unit have the improved Cummins power units. *R. O. Tuck/DCG*

YSTRAD MYNACH was the first station north of Caerphilly when the RR line opened in 1858. Originally the line was single throughout, but with increased traffic it was doubled from Caerphilly in 1872. The previous year had seen a short spur opened between Ystrad Mynach South and Penallta Junctions. This provided access via the GWR's Taff Vale Extension Line to and from the proposed Taff Bargoed Joint Line to Dowlais. In addition, with running powers over the GWR route established, the RR was also given access to the valuable mineral traffic from the Aberdare area. On 30 August 1957 the 'D7' trip to Bargoed Pits was in the care of 0-6-2T No 5687. To the right of the locomotive is the line climbing up to Penallta Junction.

The sidings that once occupied the land behind the down platform have given way to the progress of nature, but the spur up from Ystrad Mynach South Junction is still in use for coal trains to and from Cwmbargoed at the head of the Taff Bargoed Valley. On 2 April 1994 'Pacer' unit No 143 602 heads the 0847 Penarth to Rhymney service. *John Hodge/GPD*

HENGOED LOW LEVEL (1): In 1957 British Railways introduced the first of its Derby three-car DMUs for suburban services, and by the following year members of the South Wales allocation had been introduced on Rhymney Valley duties. Photographed at Hengoed Low Level station on 27 September 1958, the train comprised cars Nos 50080, 59030 and 50122. The initial livery was a medium shade of green with the cab fronts embellished with a yellow 'speed whisker'. Three marker lights were fitted to the cab front with a fourth set above the destination blind in the cab roof canopy. Later versions would be fitted with a two-figure route indicator below the centre window of the cab. An interesting feature of the train is the luggage van attached to the back. Above the rear of the train is the bridge carrying the Pontypool Road to Neath route over the former RR line.

Only the station footbridge had survived the passage of time when the corresponding view was recorded in April 1994. 'Pacer' unit No 143 623 is heading for Bargoed. *R. J. Buckley/GPD*

HENGOED LOW LEVEL (2): The former RR route is viewed from the High Level station on the Pontypool to Neath line in this illustration of 16 May 1952. The 'target' disc R3 above the right buffer identifies the coal train as a Rhymney-based locomotive duty. On the left through the trees can be seen the running lines of the Hengoed Loop, which linked the Rhymney to the Neath line via Loop Junction. The station sign confirms the interchange facilities available for passengers; if their connection was delayed they could retire to the Hengoed Junction Inn, where Simonds beer was on tap!

With the removal of the former railway overbridge, an exact corresponding vantage point could not be achieved to record the arrival of unit No 143 620 on a Barry Island service in April 1994. *R. C. Riley/DCG*

BARGOED: This early '60s view shows a three-car Derby-built DMU arriving at Bargoed. Just visible in the background is Bargoed South Junction signal box, which controlled the junction where the B&MR line crossed from the east side of the valley to join the RR tracks. The line to the right of the DMU would access the outer face of the up island platform used by the trains from Newport that would continue north for Brecon via the Bargoed-Rhymney line. Bargoed

Colliery was the scene of a world record in 1909, when 4,020 tons of coal were raised in a single shift. As well as the production record, the colliery had the less auspicious record of producing the largest spoil tip in the South Wales coalfield.

Production at the colliery ceased in 1978, and as part of an ongoing scheme to improve the landscape of the upper Rhymney Valley, considerable work has been undertaken to reduce the profile of the tip. On 18 March 1995 units Nos 150 278 and 143 606 leave Bargoed with the 1210 Rhymney to Penarth service. *John Hodge/GPD*

41

BARGOED PITS: The upper section of the Rhymney Valley had three mineral-only lines, the shortest of which was only 34 chains in length and served Bargoed Colliery, which had been opened in 1897 by the Powell Duffryn Steam Coal Company. On 27 April 1957 ex-RR Class 'R' No 38 approaches its destination with the 'D7' trip working, and provides an interesting contrast in 0-6-2T designs with the ex-GWR standard '5600' Class version represented by No 5650 on the Rhymney 'R2' duty, waiting for the road down the valley.

When visited in April 1995, a new road development to provide a bypass for Bargoed was under construction, and mature trees now cover the spoil tip that still dominates the background. 'Sprinter' unit No 150 270 is at the rear of the 0847 Penarth to Rhymney Valley Lines service in the background. *R. O. Tuck/GPD*

TIR-PHIL: BR Derby-built Class 116 set No C335 of 1957 vintage was recorded at Tir-Phil platform on 14 September 1979 while working the 1008 Penarth to Rhymney. At this stage of the line's history, local services, especially in the upper Rhymney, were well into decline with passenger usage over the previous decade reduced by over 50 per cent. Closure of this section of the route was even considered, with little interest shown by BR in promoting local travel by rail. Injudicious pruning of the once regular-interval service also took place, especially during the winter months.

Fortunately, the next decade was to witness a far more positive approach following the business sectorisation of British Rail. Local Provincial BR management worked in close co-operation with both Mid and South Glamorgan County Councils to better promote the local railways. The first trials in the Valleys using Class 150 'Sprinter' units were undertaken in 1985, and by 1992 the Class 143 'Pacers' had arrived to enable the replacement of the last of the ageing first-generation DMU stock to be completed. Our view on Good Friday 1995 shows that a light sprinkling of snow had coated this area of the valley, and 'Pacer' unit No 143 603 has a passenger awaiting its arrival. *Brian Morrison/GPD*

RHYMNEY (1): Our rainswept view of the south end of Rhymney station on 10 May 1952 shows a '5600' Class locomotive setting off down the valley. On the left is the GWR signal box that was constructed about 1936, and behind the timber-built cabin was the original RR stone-built three-road shed that dated from about 1860. The MPD allocation at nationalisation comprised 17 locomotives, the majority being either ex-RR or GWR 0-6-2 tanks.

Closed in March 1965, the shed buildings were demolished although the adjacent sidings have remained in use for the stabling of the diesel train units overnight and at weekends. Although only the down platform is now used, the station buildings on both platforms have survived and are clearly visible on either side of 'Pacer' unit No 143 603, which is setting off for Penarth on a sunny spring morning in 1995. *R. C. Riley/D. E. Moon*

RHYMNEY (2): The north end of Rhymney station on 1 August 1953 provides the splendid sight of a brace of ex-RR 0-6-2 tanks. These Hudswell Clarke engines were built in 1921 and RR No 38, as GWR No 81, received a Standard Swindon No 10 taper boiler in 1929, while No 79 (RR 36) retained its Rhymney boiler until 1949. The 2 miles of single track to Rhymney Bridge was opened in September 1871 in a joint venture with the LNWR, giving the latter company direct access for goods traffic to and from Cardiff. Although through freight working had ceased in 1933, passenger services lasted until September 1953, with five trains in each direction being provided on weekdays only.

A feature of the need to strengthen Valley Lines services on rugby international days in 1995 was the provision of two locomotive-hauled train formations to operate on the Rhymney Valley route. On 18 March Class 47/4 No 47524 stands at the rear of the 1111 service to Cardiff, with Class 37/0 No 37178 operating at the other end of the top-and-tail formation. *W. Potter/GPD*

The Taff Vale Railway - Cardiff to Taffs Well

CARDIFF BUTE ROAD (1) was known originally as Cardiff Dock station and was the southern terminus of the Taff Vale Railway (TVR) when it opened on 8 October 1840. Following the Grouping, major rebuilding work was completed and the station was renamed Bute Road by the GWR in July 1924. Our view looking north was taken in 1960 and shows a '5600' Class tank locomotive approaching, while to the right sister locomotive No 5655 is stabled at the head of a rake of empty stock.

The goods facilities were closed in March 1965 and considerable rationalisation of the railway infrastructure had been completed by the end of that decade. One platform face eventually proved sufficient for British Rail's operational requirements and the station was re-named Cardiff Bay at a ceremony on 26 September 1994. Our

corresponding view of 15 April 1995 illustrates the solitary running line remaining with 'Sprinter' unit No 150 276 departing with the 1206 shuttle service to Queen Street. *John Hodge/GPD*

CARDIFF BUTE ROAD (2): This 1960 view of the station shows a six-car DMU formation awaiting departure for Rhymney, with a steam-hauled service having just arrived at the adjacent platform. Visible on the right is the original main station building constructed by the TVR in the early 1840s. Until new and more spacious offices were completed at Queen Street in 1862, the station building contained the main offices of the TVR, including the board room.

During the '60s the station building was vacated and soon became derelict. However, when the Butetown Historic Railway Society was established in 1979, the former TVR premises were restored and they feature in our corresponding view of April 1995. Pending its transfer to Barry, the Vale of Glamorgan Railway Company began operating steam-hauled trains over a short section of track in 1994, and their locomotive *Sir Gomer* is at the rear of Class 108 DMU trailer car No 54279. *John Hodge/GPD*

CARDIFF QUEEN STREET (1): Originally known as Cardiff TVR station, re-construction was completed in 1887, when the Queen Street name was adopted. Our view taken from the south-east side of the site on 16 May 1952 shows '5600' Class 0-6-2T No 5677 with a down passenger working beneath the TVR train shed. Further re-construction work had been undertaken in 1907 and again in the 1920s, when the Rhymney Valley services were diverted to use the station. The additional facilities added to the east side of the original site can be clearly seen in this photograph.

In contrast, our view of the site in April 1995 shows the infrastructure both simplified and modernised. The railway offices of Brunel House tower over the east side of this key commuter station, served by the majority of the network of Valley Lines services. 'Sprinter' unit No 150 278 arrives with a Treherbert working. *R. C. Riley/GPD*

CARDIFF QUEEN STREET (2): For our second illustration we take you beneath the TVR train shed and record the arrival at the former platform 1 of a typical Rhondda Valley DMU service to Treherbert on 26 May 1966.

When the major reconstruction work was completed in 1973, the former platforms 1 and 2 on the west side of the station were abandoned and services were concentrated on the central island platform. Our April 1995 view from the same location shows that trees, shrubs and potted daffodils have replaced platform trolleys and passengers. 'Pacer' unit No 143 616 is about to head up the Rhymney Valley to Bargoed. *R. L. Masterman/DCG*

CATHAYS, WOODVILLE ROAD HALT was opened as a single platform on the up (northbound) side of the TVR line on 2 July 1906. Passengers wishing to travel into Cardiff would have to catch an up auto-train to Maindy Halt, then travel south on the return working. Woodville Road Halt is visible on the left of this photograph taken on 26 September 1957, which also shows ex-RR 0-6-2T No 38 entering Salisbury Road Sidings with the 'D10' working from Nantgarw.

Closed to passenger services on 15 September 1958, no trace of the former platform is visible in our April 1995 view of the location. The former sidings have given way to commercial units and a car park. Class 143 unit No 143 602 is approaching Cathays station with a Barry Island service. Opened in October 1983, Cathays proved an immediate success by attracting considerable new passenger business, being ideally sited for commuters heading for the University and commercial centre to the north of the City. *R. O. Tuck/DCG*

CATHAYS WORKS was established by the TVR in 1846 as the Company's principal carriage and wagon construction works. The Works and associated sidings occupied an 11-acre site on the down side of the TVR main line. Our early '60s view of the south end of the Works site shows a six-car DMU formation heading into Cardiff. Crockherbtown signal box is on the right, and to the left of the running lines are the tracks that accessed Cathays MPD.

The August 1994 view shows Barry Island-bound unit No 150 265. The main line provides the only remaining operational railway infrastructure, with the UCW Cardiff University occupying the former MPD land. The Works by this time was only undertaking repair work on engineering wagons and was set to close by the end of the year. *John Hodge/DCG*

CATHAYS MPD was the largest motive power depot on the Taff Vale Railway. Opened in 1884, the shed buildings provided ten roads under twin bays. During 1937/8 the five-road bay nearest to the main line was cut back to form open sidings with a repair shop at the rear. At nationalisation the allocation of 53 locomotives comprised in the main ex-TVR and GWR 0-6-2 tanks, with a number of auto-fitted Pannier tanks for use on local passenger duties. Our view of the depot on a dull 3 October 1954 shows the main shed and repair shop structures and illustrates a selection of the tank engines based there.

In 1959 the depot was partly divided to cope with an allocation of diesel multiple units, and two years later the remaining steam locomotives were transferred to Radyr. Closure of the depot came in November 1964. Our April 1994 visit to the site confirmed the redevelopment undertaken by UCW Cardiff University. To the right through the trees are the houses of Colum Road that provide a physical link between the pair of illustrations. *W. Potter/DCG*

THE ROATH BRANCH was opened by the TVR on 23 April 1888 to provide direct access to the newly opened Roath Dock. The branch was 5 miles in length and left the TVR main line on the down side just south of Llandaff to loop to the east of Cardiff before crossing the South Wales main line to the west of Pengam Junction. Our view of 25 February 1948 illustrates a typical mineral train comprising open timber-bodied wagons on the branch near Allensbank Road.

The branch was closed on 4 May 1968 and most of the northern section of the former track alignment was to disappear under the A48 Eastern Avenue Expressway constructed to link through to the M4 Motorway. *Ian L. Wright/DCG*

RADYR: On 4 April 1957 '5600' Class 0-6-2T No 6684 takes the Up Relief line with a typical train of empty mineral wagons from Radyr Yard. As well as the coal traffic from the collieries served by the former TVR routes from the Rhondda, Cynon and Taff valleys, Radyr Yard also received traffic off the former RR system via Walnut Tree Junction. However, the decline in coal exports and the closure of the collieries, coupled with the introduction of through coal workings from colliery to power station, saw activity at Radyr decline through the '60s and '70s.

The view from the station footbridge in May 1994 shows a 'Pacer' unit approaching from the City Line. The former up sidings had been removed in 1983 to enable 'park and ride' facilities to be provided. A brief coal traffic renaissance was seen in 1989, when Radyr Yard was used as a gathering point for South Wales Speedlink Coal services, but this work moved to East Usk Yard near Newport in 1990, and by the time of our 1994 visit the Yard had finally closed. *John Hodge/DCG*

PENTYRCH CROSSING was the site of a rail level crossing where an early industrial tramroad that pre-dated the TVR crossed the main line and served the Melingriffith Tin Plate Works. It was here that the TVR opened a station in October 1840, which was closed in June 1863 when Radyr station was opened. On 17 February 1962 the 2.30 pm Treherbert to Barry Island DMU was photographed passing Pentyrch station house. The leading power car is crossing the tramroad rails that passed behind Pentyrch Crossing Signal Box.

Following the closure of the private tramroad in 1962, Pentyrch Crossing box was taken out of use in October of that year. Our spring 1994 pho-tograph shows the former station house still in use. A Merthyr 'Sprinter' service formed by unit No 150 281 heads towards Taffs Well. Castell Coch is just visible above the roof of the old TVR building. *A. F. Smith, Peter Rowe (Printers)/D. E. Moon*

THE TAFF GAP is a narrow section of the Taff Vale where canal, river, road and railways once squeezed through the natural constriction that was in due course to be crossed by the Barry Railway on the impressive Walnut Tree Viaduct. On 8 August 1951 '5600' Class 0-6-2T No 6608 drifts down the Taff Vale line with a coal train heading for Radyr Yard. In the Cardiff Valleys Division, the white metal disc fixed on the lamp bracket above the right-hand buffer carried the 'target' number, normally comprising a single letter and number combination; the letter denoted the starting point of the working and also normally identified the home shed of the engine working that particular train, while the number denoted the engine diagram. In this case 'target' 'Y23' identifies the train as a Radyr Junction working.

On 9 May 1995 unit No 150 276 approaches Taffs Well with the 1427 Barry Island to Treherbert Valley Lines service. Just visible above the concrete road bridge at the edge of the trees on the left is one of the remaining piers of the former viaduct. *W. Potter/DCG*

TAFFS WELL: The clean rails illustrated in our 1980 view of Taffs Well confirm that coal traffic was then still operating via Walnut Tree Junction and the route to Penrhos Upper Junction. Having called at Taffs Well, Class 116 set No C316 heads down the Taff Vale for Cardiff Central. Introduced in 1957, many of these suburban three-car units were upgraded in the late '70s, and when they re-appeared had been repainted in the blue and white livery. This was, however, short-lived, and all-over blue was applied in due course. Just visible behind the station footbridge is the main station building on the down platform.

On Monday 30 May 1994 'Sprinter' unit No 150 270 departs with the 1350 Merthyr Tydfil to Penarth service. The original Taff Vale signal box still presides over train movements, but these are now restricted to the former TVR main line, Walnut Tree Junction having been consigned to history. The former station building has been replaced by a shelter, a car park occupies the former RR trackbed, and even the span of the station footbridge has been reduced to cross only the remaining running lines. *R. L. Masterman/DCG*

Taff Vale to Penarth and Sully

PENARTH NORTH CURVE, CARDIFF: Before we continue on to Pontypridd, we will deal with the former TVR route from Cardiff to Penarth and Sully. The Penarth Railway was opened for traffic in August 1859 from Penarth Branch Junction, Radyr, to the Penarth Tidal Harbour. The line to Penarth Dock opened in 1865 and provided the TVR with a much needed alternative outlet for the ever-growing coal traffic. On 24 September 1960 0-6-2T No 5614 sets off from Penarth Curve sidings *en route* to the Rhondda Valley. In the background is Penarth Curve North Junction signal box, and to the left are the carriage sheds on the south side of Cardiff Canton Depot.

The City Line was opened to passenger services in October 1987, with stations at Ninian Park, Waugran, Fairwater and Danescourt provided on the line that loops to the west of the City to Radyr. Unit No 150 276 has worked down from Coryton, via Cardiff Queen Street and Central stations, and is *en route* to Radyr via the City Line in this 1995 view. Provincial train units operated by South Wales and Western Cross Country and the Cardiff Valleys Operating Unit are now maintained under contract at the Canton Depot. *John Hodge/B. Cole*

COGAN JUNCTION was a hive of activity in the boom years of coal traffic to Penarth Docks. In this view of the junction taken in the early '60s the sheer size of the original Taff Vale signal box provides a measure of the scale of railway activity once supervised here. In front of the TVR structure was the GWR replacement signal box, constructed in 1926. At the head of the diverted passenger service from West Wales is 'Hymek' diesel-hydraulic No D7035. The 'Hymeks' were a regular sight on both London expresses and cross-country workings to Portsmouth following their introduction in 1961.

Remodelling and re-signalling of Cogan Junction was undertaken in 1967, when the lines to Penarth Docks were taken out of use and the line to Penarth (Town) singled. Our corresponding view of May 1995 shows 'Sprinter' unit No 150 268 heading for Barry Island. In the background is the elevated road that now provides access to the redeveloped Cardiff Bay area, and visible beneath the bridge on the east bank of the Ely River are the timber remnants of the former Victoria Wharf, which was once part of the facilities at Ely Tidal Harbour. *John Hodge/GPD*

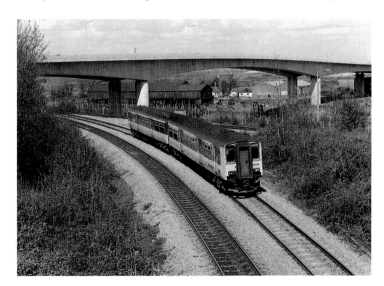

DINGLE ROAD PLATFORM was opened in 1904 to cater for the increased passenger potential on this section of the Penarth line. Penarth was a growing community, being a well-situated dormitory town for businessmen working in Cardiff. In October 1922 the GWR changed the suffix to Halt and this was retained in the title until it was officially dropped by BR in May 1969. Our view taken from a six-car DMU formation in April 1968 shows the basic passenger facilities, comprising a timber shelter on the up platform.

Our visit to Dingle Road 26 years later shows a two-car Class 143 'Pacer' unit sufficient for the passenger service requirements. On 6 April 1994 unit No 143 602 arrives with the 1247 Treherbert to Penarth service. *R. L. Masterman/GPD*

PENARTH TOWN: The Penarth Extension Railway opened on 20 February 1878 as a branch from Cogan Junction to Penarth Town. Our view of the latter station on 8 July 1967 shows Motor Brake Second single-car unit No W55019 (later Class 122) waiting to depart with the 1205 service to Cadoxton. When the Penarth branch was singled in February 1967, only the up platform at Penarth was left in use, and stop blocks were placed to divide the branch into two separate sections; these are visible behind the unit. The Cardiff section was controlled from Cardiff panel signal box, while the Cadoxton section retained double-track operation with semaphore signalling.

Following closure of the down-side platform, that side of the station site saw commercial use until, in 1990, the building and canopy were dismantled. Our view of April 1994 shows the new office development now occupying the site. Hidden behind the fence in the remaining single platform is unit No 143 609, waiting to depart for Treherbert. The pattern of services in 1995 provided departures for Treherbert, Merthyr Tydfil and Rhymney during each hour on weekdays. *Hugh Ballantyne/GPD*

ALBERTA PLACE was one of a trio of Railcar Platforms opened by the TVR in 1904 to provide additional passenger facilities near Penarth, following the considerable growth in the local population during the final two decades of the 19th century. However, by the time of nationalisation passenger loadings were in decline and in the '50s and '60s passenger traffic receipts west of Penarth fell markedly with only summer weekend traffic to the seashore at Lavernock and Swanbridge bolstering revenue. On 6 May 1967 single-car unit No W55026 was recorded working the 1.05 pm Penarth to Cadoxton service. These Class 121 Pressed Steel Company railcars were built in 1960 and were similar to the earlier Gloucester Railway Carriage & Wagon Company Class 122 versions (shown at Penarth), which were built in 1958. Comparison of the units shows that the later-built Class 121s were fitted with a four-character route indicator above the cab.

Passenger services west of Penarth were withdrawn with effect from 6 May 1968, and our view of the site in April 1994 shows Scots pine trees now well established opposite the houses of Sully Terrace. The Archer Road bridge is barely visible through the distant trees. *Hugh Ballantyne/GPD*

Past and Present Colour

South Wales
Part 2

RUMNEY RIVER BRIDGE: A strong cross-wind carries the exhaust of ex-LMSR Stanier '8F' No 48109 conveniently away to provide an unrestricted view of the assortment of bauxite-liveried vans that make up this eastbound fitted freight. Dominating the skyline of this view of 22 April 1963 near Rumney River Bridge is Roath Power Station.

In October 1991 British Rail Parcels Group launched a new specialist division called Rail Express Systems (RES), a trainload operation for the movement of bulk letters and parcels. A new corporate identity was also adopted with a dedicated fleet of locomotives and vans being painted in the RES colour scheme, based on the existing Royal Mail Travelling Post Office (TPO) livery. On Thursday 24 March 1994 Class 47/4 No 47543 passes the same location with 3V50, the MX 0500 Crewe to Cardiff and Bristol Mail. Although sporting the revised livery, the locomotive has not received its full RES branding. Of note is the assortment of van liveries providing a range of the colours used over two decades of operation. They include corporate blue, then blue and grey, as well as the TPO and latest RES variants.
Alan Jarvis/Don Gatehouse

PENGAM JUNCTION: A summer Saturday in June 1963 and an ex-GWR 'County' Class 4-6-0 passes the Up Yard at Pengam with a Cardiff to Paignton working. On the right 'Hall' Class 4-6-0 No 6985 *Parwick Hall* shunts wagons in the Yard. The Hawksworth 'Counties' were introduced in 1945 and represented the GWR's final variety of 4-6-0 design to emerge from Swindon prior to nationalisation. They were not regarded as a particular success and only 30 of these mixed traffic locomotives were built. Their working life was relatively short, and by 1962 the first withdrawals had taken place, with the last of the Class withdrawn in 1964. Unlike the majority of ex-GWR Classes, none were preserved.

By way of contrast, the Brush/Sulzer mixed traffic locomotives were first introduced in 1962 and with over 500 examples built, the Class 47s represent the most successful and versatile Type 4 diesel-electric design to operate on British Railways. On 24 March 1994 Class 47/8 No 47849 powers the 0748 Swansea to York InterCity service away from Cardiff. The locomotive carries InterCity livery but not the sector branding and Swallow motif. *Alan Jarvis/Don Gatehouse*

CARDIFF CENTRAL was, until re-named in 1966, known as Cardiff General. Our April 1961 view of the east end of the station shows 'Castle' Class No 5081 *Lockheed Hudson* arriving with a down passenger service. To the left, waiting with a train of tank wagons on the up through line, is '7200' Class 2-8-2T No 7206. When Cardiff General station was rebuilt in the early 30's, two new power boxes were opened and the semaphore signalling was replaced by colour lights. This picture shows a gantry of the colour light signals above the locomotives. Although they replaced mechanically operated signal arms, the colour aspects of the lights were simply designed to be understood by drivers in the same way as semaphore Home and Distant signals. Visible on the right is Cardiff East power box, opened in 1934. It was equipped with electric interlocking systems and miniature levers, but did not provide automatic route setting for train movements.

The signalling at Cardiff was totally renewed with the commissioning of the Cardiff 'panel' in March 1966, when multi-aspect signalling (MAS) was introduced. Our March 1995 view of the east end of the station shows power car No 43190 at the rear of a lunchtime departure for London Paddington. *Alan Jarvis/Don Gatehouse*

ROATH BRANCH JUNCTION signal box is visible in the middle distance of this April 1961 view of College Road Sidings, Llandaff. The former TVR Roath branch left the main line here to sweep to the north-east of Cardiff and access the Queen Alexandra and Roath Docks area. In the left foreground a '5700' Class 0-6-0 Pannier tank approaches the junction with a train of empty mineral wagons.

Following the closure of the Roath branch in 1968, the numerous acres of former railway land were cleared, sold and in due course re-developed. Our visit to the location on Saturday 15 April 1995 found no visible trace of the former sidings and busy junction. 'Sprinter' unit No 150 278 passes with the 1600 Treherbert to Barry Island Valley Lines service. *Alan Jarvis/Don Gatehouse*

PENARTH: The train crew relax and chat in the shade of the station canopy prior to returning to Cardiff Clarence Road in this 1954 illustration of the former TVR station at Penarth Town. Auto-fitted '6400' Class 0-6-0PT No 6435 will propel the non-corridor coach and auto-trailer combination on the return working via Cardiff Riverside.

The scene 40 years later shows that only the former up platform is now required for passenger services, and commercial premises have been built on the site of the former down platform. Behind the fencing a Class 143 'Pacer' unit awaits its departure time for Treherbert via Cardiff Central. As was the case in our earlier illustration, the platform seat is occupied, as passengers enjoy the afternoon sun before joining the train. *Alan Jarvis/Geoff Dowling*

RHOOSE: The signalman observes the passing of green-liveried BR Standard Class '3' tank No 82042 with a train of empty mineral wagons in this September 1960 view of Rhoose level crossing. The signal box, sited at the east end of the up platform of Rhoose station, also controlled access to and from the nearby cement works.

The automatic barriers that guard the level crossing are now under the control of the signal box at Aberthaw. Apart from the MGR coal traffic to and from Aberthaw Power Station, the Vale of Glamorgan route sees little activity, apart from the periods when the line is used for diversions when engineering work is being undertaken on the South Wales Main Line. A diverted London-bound HST service passes the site in May 1995. *Alan Jarvis/D. E. Moon*

ELY: The premises of a local brewery dominate the background of this 31 May 1963 view of Ely. An ex-GWR '2800' Class rumbles through with a train of 27 empty mineral wagons. On the right a rake of loaded coal wagons stands on the line that provided access to the goods yard. In the background Ely signal box is visible and beyond it and to the rear of the train the footbridge at Ely Main Line station can be seen. The station had been closed in 1962, following the withdrawal of the last local passenger workings to the west of Cardiff.

The brewery and railway station at Ely have been consigned to history and only the row of garages to the left of HST power car No 43040 provides a physical point of reference to link our corresponding view of 21 April 1995. *Alan Jarvis/Don Gatehouse*

TONDU was a focal point for railway traffic to and from the Mid-Glamorgan valleys, and a strategic location for the GWR to site a motive power depot. Set in the triangle of running lines that inter-linked the Llynvi and Ogmore Vale routes with the junction for either Bridgend or Porthcawl, this Dean standard roundhouse depot was opened in 1889. Our illustration of 29 August 1962 shows '5700' Class 0-6-0PT No 3616 passing Tondu Middle signal box with a Llynvi Valley service from Blaengwynfi to Bridgend. By that time the original slate shed roof had been replaced by corrugated sheeting.

Tondu shed closed in February 1964 and the buildings were demolished. On 8 June 1993 Class 37/7 No 37897 eases its train of loaded MEA wagons forward to take the line westwards for Margam with the 1015 return working from Pontycymmer to Jersey Marine Steel Supply. Although the railway infrastructure had been reduced to a shadow of its former self, passenger services were re-introduced to Maesteg in 1992 and coal traffic was still to be seen passing Tondu signal box in 1995. *Alan Jarvis/Geoff Dowling*

SULLY: Through passenger services between Penarth and Cadoxton on the Barry Railway commenced on 22 May 1890. Throughout the pre-Grouping and subsequent GWR eras, the pattern of passenger train workings remained largely unaltered, with services from the Taff Vale and local services from Cardiff terminating at Penarth, with further local workings to and from Cadoxton. However, the increasing competition from public and private road transport took its toll and by the time of nationalisation, passenger levels west of Penarth had fallen considerably. In an effort to revitalise passenger usage, British Railways re-scheduled services in 1953 to provide more through workings between Barry Island and Cardiff. On 21 May 1958 0-6-0PT No 8780 catches the low evening sun as it sets off from Sully with the 6.36 pm Barry Island to Cardiff Queen Street service.

Sully closed for goods traffic by October 1963 and the station closed completely following the withdrawal of passenger services in May 1968. Sold for re-development, the goods yard and station area have in turn been built on and our corresponding view of early 1995 shows that the transformation of the former railway land was nearing completion. *John Hodge/DCG*

The PC&N route from Caerphilly to Pontypridd

PENRHOS UPPER JUNCTION was located in the hills to the east of Nantgarw and was the focal point of three railways. The Pontypridd, Caerphilly & Newport Railway was built with the objective of providing an alternative outlet for coal from the Rhondda Valley to Newport for shipment, and it opened its line from Pontypridd to Penrhos for freight traffic in July 1884. The Barry Railway arrived from Tynycaeau Junction in August 1901 and in January 1905 opened its Rhymney Extension from Penrhos Lower Junction to cross the then six established lines via a new viaduct. Our view overlooking Penrhos Upper Junction on 4 October 1957 shows '5700' Class No 3717 coming off the PC&N line on the right. The RR lines drop away down the 'Big Hill' to Taffs Well in the centre, and diverging to the left of the signal box are the Barry lines to Penrhos Lower.

The former RR tracks were the last to be lifted, following the closure of this line in 1982. Our view in May 1994 shows the inevitable advance of nature, with the former Barry and Rhymney track alignments highlighted by the sun reflecting off the pools of rain water. The abandoned piers of the former Rhymney Extension line remain as monuments to a by-gone era. *R. O. Tuck/DCG*

NANTGARW: The PC&N was absorbed in 1897 by the Alexandra (Newport & South Wales) Dock & Railway, later to be known as the ADR. Passenger services between Pontypridd and Newport, via Caerphilly and Machen, had been introduced on 28 December 1887. The communities along the east side of the Taff Vale were served by a series of ground level halts, and our early '50s view of Nantgarw illustrates the facilities once provided. Auto-fitted Pannier tank No 6438 of Abercynon shed approaches with a single trailer *en route* to Machen.

Passenger services over the line were withdrawn in September 1956 and goods traffic south of Glyntaff ended in the New Year of 1967. With the railway infrastructure removed, the alignment now serves as part of the Taff Trail and can be enjoyed by walkers and cyclists, as our May 1994 illustration confirms. *Rev R. W. A. Jones/DCG*

GROESWEN HALT has two passengers awaiting the arrival of '6400' Class No 6402 in this early '50s view. Just visible to the right of the locomotive is the brickwork that survived the demolition of the former hipped-roof ADR signal box that once stood on the site. The train comprises an ex-Rhymney Open 3rd next to the engine and an ex-GWR trailer at the rear. Services over the line remained relatively unaltered for several generations, comprising seven return trips between Pontypridd and Caerphilly on weekdays, with an additional two late evening trips on Saturdays.

The former Halt site now provides a picnic area for the benefit of users of the Taff Trail, as our photograph of May 1994 illustrates. *Rev R. W. A. Jones/GPD*

PC&N JUNCTION, PONTYPRIDD: Although the founder company was absorbed into the ADR in 1897, the PC&N initials remained on display at Pontypridd for well over half a century, and into British Railways' ownership. This view of 0-6-2T locomotive No 6691 at the south end of Pontypridd station shows the 'PC&N Junction' signal box on the left. Beyond the signals in the distance the PC&N tracks swing to the left to cross the Taff Vale and continue south to Penrhos and Caerphilly. The tracks bearing to the right are the former TVR lines to Treforest.

No trace of the former junction has survived the major works undertaken in connection with a road-widening scheme to relieve traffic congestion in Pontypridd, as our August 1994 illustration confirms. Setting off down the Taff Vale is 'Pacer' unit No 143 611. *D. Mathew/DCG*

Taff Vale from Pontypridd to Merthyr

PONTYPRIDD (1): Having reached Pontypridd, we will continue up the Taff Vale, dealing with the branch lines as well as the line to Merthyr Tydfil. Called Newbridge station when the TVR opened its line in October 1840, it was re-built and re-named Pontypridd in 1891. Originally the station comprised separate up and down platforms, but major reconstruction work was undertaken by the GWR in 1907 to produce the single long island platform and extended main roof illustrated in our 1954 view. Abercynon locomotive No 6438 awaits departure for Caerphilly with an auto-train service as part of Abercynon duty 'JF'.

With the rationalisation of Valley services completed during the '60s, tracks were removed from the down

side of the island platform, and from 1970 the up platform face was used by all trains. However, with the increased frequency of trains introduced in the late '80s, the bi-directional platform operations proved inadequate to cope with the number of services passing through Pontypridd. Indeed, certain Merthyr services had to run through using the freight relief lines. Eventually, a new platform was built on the west side of the station site and our view of 13 August 1994 shows unit No 150 275 approaching the new up platform with the 1527 Penarth to Merthyr Tydfil service. *A. Jarvis/DCG*

PONTYPRIDD (2): A busy scene at the north end of Pontypridd station on 26 July 1952. The 5.34 pm auto-train for Old Ynysybwl Halt is waiting in the bay platform, with Pannier tank No 5421 at the head of a former steam railmotor trailer. On the left, ex-TVR Class 'A' 0-6-2T No 371 is on a Merthyr Tydfil working, while on the right ex-GWR 0-6-2T No 6661 stands in the adjoining bay platform road.

The withdrawal of the local branch services based on Pontypridd left only through workings to and from Cardiff, so the bay platforms were rendered superfluous. Our August 1995 view of the former bay platforms shows the infill undertaken, although the former platform edges were still visible. On the extreme right is the new up platform and connecting footbridge, opened in June 1991. *R. C. Riley/DCG*

YNYSYBWL: The TVR opened the Ynysybwl branch from Clydach Court Junction to Llanwonno for freight in 1885, with passenger services from Abercynon to Ynysybwl commencing in the New Year of 1890. With the opening of the Clydach Court Loop in 1900, passenger services were altered to operate to and from Pontypridd, and in October 1904 steam railcars were introduced on the branch. Ynysybwl was the only station on the line and our view of Pannier tank No 5421 on 13 May 1952 shows the single platform, with the goods yard behind the Taff Vale station building. The community had developed around the Lady Windsor Colliery, which had been sunk in 1885-6, and it was to provide an outlet for the coal raised at the colliery that the railway was built. Freight workings to Ynysybwl ceased in November 1959, leaving only the colliery to generate revenue-earning mineral traffic.

Our visit to the location in 1994 found the original TVR station building and goods shed still in use as part of commercial premises. However, the somewhat unsympathetic extension to the former station building and the collection of scrap vehicles in the surrounding yard were less pleasing to the eye. *R. C. Riley/DCG*

OLD YNYSYBWL: Barely half a mile further up the valley was Old Ynysybwl Halt. The line did continue further up the valley to Mynachdy Colliery, but beyond there the tracks had been lifted in 1938. With a rising gradient of 1 in 51, easing to 1 in 59 on the approach to the Halt, drivers could not afford to shut off steam until they had reached the platform. The passenger timetable of 1951 lists seven return trips over the branch on weekdays, with morning and late afternoon workings operated via Abercynon for the benefit of local schoolchildren. Two additional return workings were provided on Saturdays.

Passenger services were withdrawn from July 1952 and with general freight ceasing in 1959, coal traffic from Lady Windsor Colliery continued until March 1988, when production ceased. The branch was abandoned following the last coal train from the Lady Windsor site on 20 May 1988. Old Ynysybwl platform is just visible in this April 1994 view of the site. The stump of the telegraph pole and truncated base of the nameboard could still be traced on the earth mound that once formed the platform. *R. C. Riley/DCG*

CILFYNYDD: The Taff Vale Railway opened a branch to Cilfynydd in 1887 to serve Albion Colliery, and in 1900 the line was extended to join the earlier Stormstown to Llancaiach mineral line at Ynysydwr. Passenger services using steam railcars were introduced between Pontypridd and Nelson TVR stations, and Cilfynydd was one of three stations opened on the line, with Halts serving other locations. The branch was single-track, being worked by electric train staff, and near Cilfynydd an intermediate crossing loop was provided. Being sited close to the main road out from Pontypridd, Cilfynydd was also served by electric trams, and by 1932 the GWR had found the competition for passengers too one-sided and withdrew its auto-train service. On 12 July 1952 the abandoned platform at Cilfynydd was visited by enthusiasts travelling on an SLS Special comprising Pannier tank No 6423 and a pair of ex-TVR trailer cars.

The track beyond Cilfynydd had been lifted in 1936, but the remainder of the line remained in use until September 1970, when coal traffic from Albion Colliery ceased. The A470 dual carriageway has obliterated part of the branch line and our 1994 view of the school premises that now occupy land adjacent to the new road shows the terraced house backs of Cilfynydd on the hillside still providing a point of reference. *R. C. Riley/DCG*

ABERCYNON MPD was the first locomotive shed of its type to be built by the GWR in 1929, to replace the original TVR depot that stood on the same site. Under the Government's Loans & Guarantees Act (1929), financial aid was given to companies that wished to expand, thereby creating jobs to ease the high unemployment of the time. The GWR was able to use the scheme to update facilities and replace some of the pre-Grouping depots that were proving inadequate for operational needs. The allocation at Abercynon at nationalisation comprised 29 tank locomotives, principally of the 0-6-2 and 0-6-0 variety. Examples of these ex-GWR engines were on view when the depot was visited on 14 October 1962.

Closure came in November 1964, but the shed has since seen use as a foundry and was still in situ when the former railway land was visited in 1994. In the background a Class 150/2 unit approaches Abercynon from the Merthyr branch. *W. Potter/DCG*

QUAKER'S YARD LOW LEVEL (1): On 5 June 1964 '5600' Class 0-6-2T No 5641 hustles through the up platform with the 'target' 'C05' coal empties, while a six-car DMU stands at the down platform with a Merthyr to Cardiff working. Behind the DMU is the ornate TVR main station building that dated back over a century to the origins of the line.

Our April 1995 view shows the abandoned former up platform, with Penarth-bound unit No 150 269 standing adjacent to the shelter now provided for passengers on the down platform. Coal traffic can no longer be seen in this section of the Taff Vale following the closure of Merthyr Vale Colliery in June 1989. The colliery dated back to 1869 and was the oldest operational mine in the South Wales coalfield. *W. Potter/D. E. Moon*

QUAKERS YARD LOW LEVEL (2): Pannier tank No 5730 rumbles through with an up freight on 5 June 1964. The station nameboard describes the interchange facilities available with the adjacent High Level station for stations to Swansea via Aberdare and Pontypool Road via the former Taff Vale Extension route through Hengoed and Crumlin. The footbridge spanned the Low Level station site and linked through to the High Level station, the water tower of which is visible top right.

Closure of the High Level station came in June 1964 and, following clearance of the railway infrastructure, the land was sold to be used for a housing development. With the Low Level suffix no longer needed, the former TVR station is served by the Valley Lines units, and No 150 279 was photographed in May 1994 arriving with a Penarth working. *W. Potter/D. E. Moon*

MERTHYR TYDFIL HIGH STREET: The original TVR station of 1841 was at Plymouth Street, Merthyr Tydfil, but in 1877 a connecting line was built to provide access to the High Street station, where the Vale of Neath Railway had established its terminus in 1853. By the time of our 2 May 1964 illustration, alterations to the original Brunel station had already been made. Locomotive No 6606, then of Cardiff East Dock (88B), has just arrived from Cardiff General.

The final work to rationalise the station facilities and complete the replacement of the remaining Brunel structure with a modern booking office was completed in 1971. Our visit to the station on 14 April 1995 was timed to record the departure of 'Pacer' unit No 143 603 with the 1350 service to Penarth via Cardiff. By the autumn of 1995, work had commenced to construct a new station to the south of the present site to release land for a new town centre shopping development. *E. T. Gill/GPD*

80

Rhondda valleys

PORTH: Our 1963 view looking north from the station footbridge at Porth shows a Treherbert-bound DMU departing on the left, with the connecting service to Maerdy awaiting departure from the island platform on the right. The lines serving the Rhondda Fawr and Fach Valleys take their respective routes on either side of the Rhondda Fach North Junction signal box, visible beneath the road bridge.

On 13 August 1994 the driver of 'Sprinter' unit No 150 267 forming the 0930 Treherbert to Barry Island service has just surrendered the single line token at Porth. *John Hodge/DCG*

TYLORSTOWN: From Porth we will initially head up the Rhondda Fach to Maerdy. On a dull 1 March 1958 0-6-2T No 5600 of Ferndale MPD approaches Tylorstown station with a passenger service from Maerdy. On the left a sister locomotive shunts the sidings that served Ferndale No 9 Pit. Ferndale Nos 8 and 9 were the southernmost of the Ferndale Group of collieries and No 8 Pit was sunk to a depth of 456 yards in 1894. It was to develop into the largest of the Ferndale Group and in 1918 employed 1,145 men underground. The No 8 Pit had ceased production in 1935, but No 9 continued until 1960.

Demolition of the colliery site was undertaken during 1967 and our visit to the location in April 1994 revealed the customary expanse of levelled wasteland marking a former colliery site where subsequent redevelopment has not taken place. The single track of the former down line is still in situ amongst the weeds. *John Hodge/DCG*

FERNDALE MPD was built by the TVR in 1884 and was situated on the up side of the line to the north of Ferndale station and on the east bank of the River Rhondda Fach. In GWR ownership the shed was reduced from four roads to two, the turntable was removed and a corrugated awning was provided to cover the coaling road. At nationalisation the allocation comprised 13 0-6-2 tanks of either TVR or GWR origin, working principally on local coal trains and the branch passenger duties. The depot was a sub-shed to Treherbert MPD. Our view of the south end of the shed taken at the time of a depot visit in August 1956 shows a '5600' Class locomotive standing behind the ash pit on the road that ran between the main shed building and the depot offices. On the right is Maerdy Junction signal box, beyond which the single line to Maerdy continues up the valley.

Closed in September 1964, the depot site was subsequently cleared. However, our photograph taken at the location in early 1995 clearly shows the former ash pit still visible. *GPD collection/GPD*

MAERDY (1): On 6 March 1958 the 3.25 pm service to Porth sets off down the Rhondda Fach. The train comprises an all-3rd coach and, at the rear, Brake 3rd No W256W, which has been rebuilt with a driving cab and ATC fittings to enable the two-coach combination to be operated as a push-pull formation if required.

The same view some 25 years later shows Class 37/0 No 37251 at the head of a train of coal about to depart for the Phurnacite Plant at Abercwmboi. Although Abercwmboi is in an adjacent valley and less than 3 miles away from Maerdy 'as the crow flies', the train will have to run down to Pontypridd, then continue up the Taff and Cynon Valleys to reach the plant, a distance of 18 miles by rail.

Our final illustration looking down the Rhondda Fach was taken in 1994. The landscape has not changed to any great degree during the 36 years spanned by the three photographs. Only a thin scar along the valley floor now remains to mark the passing of the railway era. *R. O. Tuck/DCG (2)*

MAERDY (2): Passenger services had been introduced to serve the mining communities of the Rhondda Fach in 1889 and Maerdy station, situated at the head of the valley, was some 900 feet above sea level and the highest station on the TVR system. On 6 May 1960 the DMU shuttle service to Porth awaits departure. This service was basically of an hourly frequency on weekdays only, with 18 minutes being sufficient to for the 6-mile run to Porth, with three intermediate stops. The station site retains a wealth of former TVR architecture and on the right in front of the station building is the corrugated iron carriage shed once used to house the branch auto-train. The line to the left that runs past the signal box continues into the NCB sidings and on to the colliery beyond.

Passenger services were withdrawn on 15 June 1964. However, the branch remained open until 1986, when coal traffic from Maerdy Colliery ceased. The movement of Rhondda coal by rail dated back to the opening of the first TVR line to Dinas in 1841. The peak year of production was reached during 1913, when 9.3 million tons of coal was produced in the Rhondda Coalfield, but the cessation of coal movements from Maerdy in 1986 saw the end of railborne coal traffic in the Rhondda valleys. Our view of 1994 shows the site cleared; note the recess on the left, where the signal box once stood. *E. T. Gill/DCG*

PWLLYRHEBOG INCLINE: Returning to the Rhondda Fawr, we head north from Porth to Tonypandy. In 1863 the TVR opened this unique branch from Pwllyrhebog Branch Junction up the Clydach Vale to serve Blaenclydach Colliery. In the same year a private line was built to serve Clydach Vale Colliery and this was acquired by the TVR in 1896 and joined to the branch three years later. The branch was unique because of the mode of operation required to haul wagons up the 1 in 13 incline. The incline would be worked by two engines, both attached to a wire rope. They ran on parallel tracks and were always at the bottom or Pwllyrhebog end of the wagons. A speed limit of 5 miles per hour was imposed on engines on any part of the incline, with or without wagons attached. As well as coal, the branch handled general goods, including livestock to and from the goods station and yard at Blaenclydach. Viewed from an overbridge, looking up the gradient in August 1951, a month after closure of the line, the severity of the climb is clear to see.

Although the overbridge has been demolished and the former railway land re-profiled, our view of May 1995 can be easily matched with the earlier one by studying the structures to the rear of the terraced houses on the right. *W. Potter/GPD*

PWLLYRHEBOG MPD: For some 67 years of the incline's operation, a unique trio of specially designed 0-6-0T, TVR Class 'H', locomotives was in service. Built by Kitson & Co, TVR Nos 141-3 (GWR Nos 792-4, then BR Nos 193-5) had steeply tapered boilers to avoid the firebox crown being uncovered during operation on the steep gradient. In addition, 5 ft 3 in diameter wheels were fitted to provide ample clearance over the haulage gear. The locomotive shed was constructed close to the top of the incline and our illustration of 14 October 1949 shows the corrugated iron structure that replaced the original TVR shed. Engine No 195 is awaiting its next turn of duty. Behind the shed is the signal box that was also visible at the summit of the incline on the left of the tracks in our 1951 view of the branch. The three locomotives were allocated to Treherbert MPD and it was customary for two of them to work on the branch at a time, each being used for four weeks with two weeks off duty back at Treherbert. None of the locomotives visited Swindon Works during their working lives.

The re-profiled land and a road constructed across the former track alignment left little in the foreground to associate the two illustrations. However, a study of the background houses will provide confirmation of our tracing the location correctly. *W. Potter/DCG*

LLWYNYPIA: On 12 May 1956 0-6-0 'Dean Goods' No 2538 ambles down the Rhondda Fawr with a Gloucestershire Railway Society enthusiasts' special. The third running line is a Down Relief road used for mineral traffic.

With a decline in both coal and local passenger traffic throughout the '60s and '70s, rationalisation of the railway infrastructure culminated in the route being singled north of Porth in March 1981. However, as elsewhere on the Valley Lines network, the 1980s produced better promotion of local rail travel and this saw a marked upturn in the Rhondda's fortunes. Ultimately, new stations were constructed in the late '80s, and a half-hourly frequency of service was introduced in the autumn of 1986 following the opening of a new station at Ystrad Rhondda and the installation of a crossing loop. Our view of the same location in August 1994 shows the fixed distant board that cautions northbound drivers on the approach to Ystrad Rhondda. The unit, No 150 269, is working the 1500 Treherbert to Barry Island service. *R. O. Tuck/DCG*

TREHERBERT: The TVR mineral line from Dinas to Treherbert was completed in August 1856, but passenger services were not introduced until January 1863. The Rhondda & Swansea Bay Railway arrived from the north via the 3,443-yards-long Rhondda Tunnel in July 1890. The station at Treherbert comprised an island platform and was served by Cardiff trains in the one direction and Swansea services in the other. Our view of the station taken on 12 May 1956 shows a Cardiff service awaiting departure behind a '5600' Class locomotive, while on the right is the 'Dean Goods' again, which has just arrived with the enthusiasts' special.

In an effort to save on tunnel maintenance costs, passenger services via the Rhondda Tunnel ceased from 26 February 1968, when a bus service was introduced between Treherbert and Cymmer in lieu of the trains. The tunnel was closed officially at the end of 1970. On Monday 30 August 1993 'Sprinter' unit No 150 272 awaits departure with the 1647 service to Penarth. *W. Potter/D. E. Moon*

Barry Railway lines

CREIGIAU: The Barry Railway line north of Cadoxton was primarily built to provide a direct rail link between the Rhondda coalfield at Trehafod and Barry Docks, just under 19 miles to the south. The route passed through mainly undeveloped rural country, and when passenger services between Barry and Pontypridd were introduced on 16 March 1896, Creigiau was one of the communities served by an intermediate station on the line. Our view of the station on 26 August 1958 shows auto-fitted Pannier tank No 6435 with the two-coach train operated between Cardiff and Pontypridd, via St Fagans. The locomotive carries a disc denoting duty 'JB', and this diagram of passenger duties was undertaken by an Abercynon-based engine. The first service of a weekday duty ran from Pontypridd, via St Fagans, to arrive at Cardiff Clarence Road at 8.30. Following the completion of two return workings to Penarth, a lunchtime return working to Pontypridd was made. Then a further three afternoon trips to Penarth would be undertaken before the final evening service from Clarence Road departed

at 5.31 pm to return to Pontypridd. On Saturdays, only the morning services would be undertaken, the duty ending with the 12.45 Clarence Road to Pontypridd.

The duties of auto-train 'JB' operated between September 1953 and 1962, when the associated passenger services were withdrawn. Through passenger services between Barry and Pontypridd lasted a further two years and the route closed to mineral traffic in June 1963. Visited in May 1995, the station site was somewhat overgrown, but the platforms were still in situ. *Hugh Ballantyne/DCG*

ABOVE NANTGARW: The Barry Railway line from Tynycaeau to Penrhos was opened for mineral traffic on 1 August 1901. Although it remained primarily a freight-only route throughout its existence, it was used on summer Sundays and Bank Holidays by excursion trains from the Valleys *en route* to Barry Island. On 17 May 1959 a Sunday excursion from Dowlais Cae Harris to Barry Island in the care of '5600' Class 0-6-2T No 5652 coasts down from Penrhos Lower Junction towards Walnut Tree Viaduct. The train would have travelled down the Taff Bargoed route to Nelson & Llancaiach, then briefly joined the Neath to Pontypool Road line to reach Ystrad Mynach via Penallta Junction. Having travelled south to Aber Junction, the train would have continued westward to Penrhos Upper Junction, where it would have joined the ex-Barry Railway line. The former Cardiff Railway line can be seen just above the train and to the left, beyond the River Taff, is the ex-TVR main line to Pontypridd. On the east side of the Taff Vale is Nantgarw Colliery and the associated Coke Works, which had been developed in the early '50s.

Since the closure of the former Barry Railway line from Penrhos Junction at the end of 1967, the tracks have been removed and the course of the railway has in the main returned to nature. Our view over Nantgarw in April 1995 shows a picnic area now occupying the former trackbed at this location. Nantgarw Colliery closed at the end of 1986, with the coke ovens closing early in the following year. The site has been cleared and redeveloped as a business park. *R. O. Tuck/GPD*

WALNUT TREE VIADUCT (1): The Nantgarw or Taff Gap at Taffs Well is a large natural geological fault in the rock barrier that marks the southern limit of the Glamorgan Coalfield. Having travelled down from Penrhos Junction on a maximum falling gradient of 1 in 81, trains heading for Barry would cross the Taff Vale 120 feet above the tracks of the TVR on the 1,548-foot-long Walnut Tree Viaduct, which comprised seven steel lattice girder spans resting on masonry piers. Although mineral traffic to Barry via Walnut Tree Viaduct ceased on 30 March 1963, the line from Penrhos Junction to the Dolomite Works on the west side of the Taff Vale continued to be used. On 13 May 1965 '5600' Class 0-6-2T No 6672 approaches the west end of the viaduct with the 12.30 trip working from Aber Junction.

Local workings to the Dolomite Works continued until December 1967, when the line from Penrhos was closed. With the tracks lifted, the girder spans were removed in 1969 and demolition of most of the masonry piers was completed in 1973. However, as can be seen from our April 1995 view, two of the piers remain to mark the alignment of the former viaduct across the valley. *Hugh Ballantyne/GPD*

WALNUT TREE VIADUCT (2): This second view was taken on 12 May 1965 and shows '5600' Class locomotive No 6614 crossing to reach the Works siding with the Aber Junction Yard trip working. The locomotive and 11 wagons that made up the train are somewhat dwarfed by the sheer size of both the viaduct and the Dolomite Works, visible to the left. In the foreground a Mobil road tanker is parked in a layby on the old A470 Cardiff to Merthyr Tydfil road.

Our corresponding view exactly 30 years later shows the two masonry piers that survived the demolition of the viaduct. The pier on the right marks the course of the River Taff and the location of the former TVR line that runs alongside and between the river and the A470 road. The site of the former Dolomite Works has been cleared and landscaped, and the A470 has also seen considerable change, with a dual carriageway now required to cater for the demands of the volume of road traffic using this trunk route that links the towns and industries of the Cardiff Valleys with the M4 motorway. This section of the A470 road development to the north of Tongwynlais obliterated the track alignment of the former Cardiff Railway line when it was constructed.
Hugh Ballantyne/GPD

TYNYCAEAU JUNCTION: The Barry Railway lines from Trehafod on the TVR and Penrhos on the RR converged at Tynycaeau Junction, some 6 miles to the north of Cadoxton. Here also a connecting spur came up a 1 in 89 climb from the South Wales main line at St Fagans to trail into the Barry line in a northerly direction. Immediately south of the junction, goods loops were provided on both the up and down sides of the Barry line, Tynycaeau South signal box being sited at their southern end. Passing the somersault signal sited adjacent to the South signal box on 15 March 1948 with a Pontypridd to Barry service is ex-TVR 'A' Class 0-6-2T No 375.

The corresponding view taken in May 1995 shows the transformation from railway to road that has been completed in the intervening years. The alignment of the railway that ran to Creigiau has been used for the construction of an expressway leading to the M4 motorway. To the west of the dual-carriageway, the alignment of the former spur from St Fagans can still be traced, and to the north of the former junction site trees mark the alignment of the former Barry line that heads away north-eastwards towards the Taff Gap. *Ian L. Wright/DCG*

DROPE JUNCTION was located to the south of the South Wales Main Line and just under 4 miles from Cadoxton. On 6 August 1957 '5600' Class 0-6-2T No 5615 passes with an empty stock working heading for Barry Island. As was the custom in the South Wales valleys, the locomotive is running bunker-first when travelling southbound. The lines to the left head westwards for approximately 2 miles and descend to make a junction with the former GWR main line close to the village of Peterston-super-Ely. The link between Drope and Peterston East Junctions opened for goods and mineral traffic on 18 July 1889; scheduled passenger services were never operated over the line.

The corresponding road overbridge provides the vantage point to illustrate the use made of the former Barry line following closure in 1963. Above the layby to the right a distant HST can be seen passing on the main line, and in the background above the train the sharp drop in the hill profile on the horizon marks the site of the Nantgarw or Taff Gap. *Ian L. Wright/DCG*

WENVOE (1): South of Drope Junction, the Barry line passed through the 1 mile 108 yards of Wenvoe Tunnel and continued down Wenvoe Bank. Drifting down towards an 'on' signal at Wenvoe on Sunday 8 June 1958, an ex-LNWR 0-8-0 had charge of the 9.15 Nantybwch to Barry Island excursion. This Tredegar-based duty was rostered for these ex-LNWR goods engines until the end of the summer season of 1958; a similar working has already been featured passing Llanbradach in the Rhymney Valley (pages 34-5). To reach the former Barry Railway lines, the train will have travelled via Aber and Penrhos Upper junctions to cross Walnut Tree Viaduct and continue via Tynycaeau Junction.

The route down from Nantybwch represented one of the most intriguing railway journeys to be undertaken from the Heads of the Valleys to the coast. Alas, the majority of the lines once used have been closed and only the sections of the former route between Ystrad Mynach and Aber Junction in the Rhymney Valley, and Cadoxton to Barry Island, remain open. As our April 1994 view of the former Wenvoe Bank illustrates, those sections of the former railway land that have not seen redevelopment have become overgrown and returned to nature. *R. O. Tuck/DCG*

WENVOE (2): Passenger services between Barry and Pontypridd commenced on 16 March 1896, and as the line only served a series of small communities, the level of service operated was never significant. In the early years after nationalisation, four return workings calling at all stations on the route were provided each week-day; a single return working to Barry Island was also operated on summer Sundays. By 1961 the level of service had declined to a single return working each morning on weekdays, with additional Barry Island services during the summer months on Sundays. On 6 August 1957 auto-fitted Prairie tank No 5527 is seen at Wenvoe with a Pontypridd service.

The station at Wenvoe closed following the withdrawal of passenger services on 10 September 1962. Viewed in April 1994, the platforms are still in situ and the main station building is in use as a private residence. The building on the former down platform has seen commercial use since the closure of the railway, and can just be seen through the growth of trees that now occupies the former trackbed. *Ian L. Wright/DCG*

CADOXTON SIDINGS (1): At Cadoxton the Barry Railway built a large expanse of reception sidings that occupied land on both sides of the running lines. It was to here that trains of loaded coal from the numerous collieries in the Welsh valleys would be brought to await onward movement to the docks for unloading, when required. Spanning the central area of the sidings was a lattice footbridge and this provided an ideal vantage point from which to observe the countless coal train movements. Our 'past' illustration of 23 July 1961 records '5600' Class 0-6-2T No 5678, in lined green livery, passing under the footbridge with a Pontypridd to Barry Island excursion. As a favour to the photographer, the signalman had also pulled off the northbound somersault signals.

  With the closure of the railway, such an expanse of level ground provided prime land for redevelopment

and, as our May 1995 illustration shows, the local children can no longer savour the sight of a passing ex-GWR tank locomotive on either a coal or excursion train. Visible in both photographs on the higher ground to the right and providing a reference point is Palmerstown House, which dates back to 1899. *Hugh Ballantyne/DCG*

CADOXTON SIDINGS (2): Our second view at Cadoxton sidings was taken from the footbridge looking south on 19 June 1960. By that time the vast majority of the sidings lay unused and it must be left to the imagination to visualise what the scene must have been like when coal exports were at their peak in 1913. During that year the Docks at Barry dealt with 11 million of the estimated 37 million tons of coal that were shipped through the South Wales ports. Heading back to Aberdare with a well-loaded train of suburban stock, ex-GWR '5600' Class No 6651 is gathering speed for the climb up Wenvoe Bank.

With the closure of the railway, the lattice footbridge was eventually removed and, in the absence of the power of levitation, we were unable to obtain the corresponding view precisely when the site was visited in May 1995. Taken from the east end of the former footbridge, the cranes at Barry Docks are still visible above the houses that now occupy the former railway land. *John Hodge/GPD*

CADOXTON station was built at the intersection of the lines from Tynycaeau and Cogan junctions, and our view from the end of the station platform in 1967 shows the lines to Cogan curving away to the right behind the former Barry Railway Cadoxton South signal box. The Class 122 single-car unit is stabled on the former Tynycaeau road between duties on the Penarth line. By this time, recovery of the sidings that once occupied the land behind the diesel unit had been completed and the footbridge that spanned the former sidings can be seen in the left distance.

'Sprinter' unit No 150 281 heads away from Cadoxton on Sunday 30 April 1995 with the 1331 Barry Island to Cardiff Central service. *R. L. Masterman/DCG*

COGAN station had opened when the Barry Railway introduced local passenger trains between Barry Docks and Cogan on 20 December 1888; services were extended to Barry Town in February 1889. Our 1960 view from the station footbridge shows D1046 *Western Marquis* passing with a diverted through service for London Paddington. The station buildings were still in use at this time and, above the locomotive, mineral wagons can be seen in the adjoining goods yard.

The goods yard closed in November 1964 and Cogan station became unstaffed from 2 February 1970. Our corresponding view of 21 April 1995 shows the simple shelters now provided on the platforms following the demolition of the former structures. Passengers are about to board 'Pacer' unit No 143 607, working the 1544 Barry Island to Aberdare service. *John Hodge/GPD*

COGAN TUNNEL is 222 yards in length and represents the only significant engineering feature on the section of line between Cogan Junction and Cadoxton. From our vantage point above the eastern portal on 3 May 1964 we see an unidentified 'Western' Class diesel-hydraulic locomotive approaching with the diverted 1500 London Paddington to Swansea service. Cogan Sidings signal box is visible on the left, controlling access to the relief lines that run through to Cogan Junction.

The extent of the tree growth has provided a natural frame for our April 1995 view of the location. 'Pacer' unit No 143 608 approaches the tunnel with the 1417 Aberdare to Barry Island service. *John Hodge/GPD*

BIGLIS JUNCTION was opened for goods traffic in December 1888 and, when introduced in the following August, permitted passenger services to and from Penarth via Sully to operate over the Barry Railway metals as far as Cadoxton. On 7 August 1957 '5600' Class 0-6-2T No 6603 has just come off the Penarth branch with an excursion *en route* to Barry Island.

The junction was taken out of use following the closure of the Penarth line in May 1968. On 6 April 1994 unit No 150 281 passes the site with the 1517 Treherbert to Barry Island service. *John Hodge/GPD*

PALMERSTOWN: On 25 May 1958 the evening sun illuminates the 7.40 pm Barry Island to Birmingham Tyseley excursion as 'Hall' Class 4-6-0 No 4965 *Rood Aston Hall* heads away from Cadoxton station.

The view taken on 6 April 1994 shows the commercial development at Palmers View Business Park that now occupies the former railway land on the down side of the running lines. The gables of the former Collis Light Engineering Works are still visible on the left, but this building has since been demolished. Private gardens now occupy the former sidings in the right foreground. Unit No 150 277 heads towards Cardiff with the 1828 Barry Island to Aberdare service. *John Hodge/GPD*

BARRY DOCKS: To cater for coal trains arriving from the Cogan direction, the Barry Railway laid reception sidings that extended between Cadoxton and Barry Docks stations. As a measure of the extent of reception lines provided for coal traffic, the sidings at Cadoxton and Barry Dock at one time aggregated to over 100 miles of track. To give direct access from the Dock Sidings to a number of the dockside coal tips, a burrowing junction was constructed in 1898/9. Our view across the sidings in 1962 shows the coal tips of No 2 Dock in the background. Emerging from the subway tunnel is ex-LMSR 2-8-0 '8F' No 48412 at the head of a Barry Dock to Oldbury phosphate train.

On 13 April 1994 Class 09 shunter No 09015 returns from the dock area to climb up to the remaining sidings in the background (since lifted). The coal tips on the north side of No 2 Dock have been removed but the cranes on the far side of the dock are still visible. *John Hodge/GPD*

107

BARRY No 2 DOCK opened in 1898 and provided 34 of the 73 acres of enclosed dock that was sited between Barry Island and the mainland. The north side of No 2 Dock was equipped with coal tips, while the south side of the dock had facilities for handling general cargo. It is this latter commodity that provides the traffic being conveyed in our 1954 view of ex-GWR '9400' Class 0-6-0PT No 8481 at the head of the 'target' 'B36' working from Barry Docks to Newtown Goods Depot, Cardiff.

Although all coal traffic has ceased, this section of the docks railway system still sees some freight activity, and on Friday 12 May 1995 Class 56 No 56113 passes the same location *en route* from Cardiff Canton Depot to collect the tank wagons that will form the evening departure for Burn Naze in the North West of England. *John Hodge/DCG*

BARRY DOCK OFFICE dominates our brace of illustrations taken from the road overlooking the west end of Barry Docks station. It was constructed as the general offices of the Barry Railway Company and was fully opened in February 1900, although it had been partly occupied from the middle of the previous year. Built of red brick and Portland stone in the Neo-Baroque Renaissance style, the original design included a clock in the south face of the building, above the boardroom, where the Board of the Barry Railway Company met on the first Friday of each month. However, the Clock Tower was added during the construction work and the date 1899 was set in stone where the original clock would have been located. On 30 April 1958 the 6.36 pm working from Barry Island to Cardiff Queen Street passes in the care of '5700' Class 0-6-0PT No 4667. Behind the signal box and to the right, coal tips in the No 1 Dock can be seen.

Between January 1922 and March 1967 the GWR, then British Railways, maintained offices in the building. However, the structure and in particular the Clock Tower suffered severe fire damage in March 1984 resulting in the reconstruction of the Tower and the provision of a new electronic clock. The restored building assumed

Grade II* listed status in July 1990 and now provides accommodation for the Headquarters of HM Customs for Wales. The clock confirms that 'Pacer' unit No 143 606 is on time as it approaches Barry Docks on 13 April 1994 with the 1605 Valley Lines service from Barry Island to Rhymney. *John Hodge/GPD*

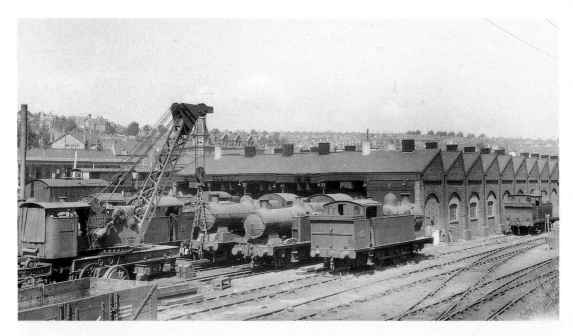

BARRY MPD: The Barry Railway established its principal motive power depot and workshops on land to the south-east of Barry Town station between 1893-7. The GWR added a new coaling stage in 1926, and it is from this vantage point that our view of the west end of the main shed was taken on 31 August 1947. When the Barry Company was merged into the GWR in 1922, it provided 148 engines, a number of which survived through into British Railways' ownership.

During its later years a new corrugated roof was added, but raised to provide addition headroom. Our January 1993 view of the Depot building shows the additional brickwork added when the original slated roof was replaced. Closed as a steam depot in September 1964, the main shed building has survived to provide workshop facilities where the South Wales fleet of coal wagons are maintained and repaired. The HAA coal hopper wagon second from the left of our picture carries the logo of a galleon in full sail, being the Depot motif applied to many of the wagons above the bodyside 'Barry' branding. *W. Potter/GPD*

BARRY JUNCTION: Just prior to the introduction of DMUs on the scheduled Valley Lines services in 1958, a typical steam-hauled formation of rolling-stock is seen leaving the Island causeway and rounding the curve at Barry Junction. The 6.30 pm Barry Island to Treherbert is approaching Barry Town station in the care of '5100' Class 2-6-2T No 5162.

The first-generation DMUs had come and gone by the time of this second view over the junction in April 1994, with two-car 'Sprinter' unit No 150 277 providing today's typical Valley Lines train formation. Introduced in 1986, the Class 150/2 units were constructed at BREL York Works for provincial commuter and cross-country services. In 1994 the Cardiff Valleys Train Operating Unit employed a dedicated fleet of 18 of these two-car units. *John Hodge/DCG*

BARRY ISLAND has for a number of generations been the destination for thousands of railway excursions bringing visitors from many parts of the UK, but in particular the Welsh valleys. The short causeway from Barry Town was opened on 3 August 1896 and the arrival of the railway enabled the resort to develop rapidly. The GWR enlarged the station in 1930 and our view on a summer evening in 1960 typifies the volume of passenger activity that would be seen on a Sunday or Bank Holiday weekend.

Peace and tranquillity better describes our view of the location on Saturday 5 March 1994, when 'Pacer' unit No 143 622 was recorded departing with the 1227 service to Aberdare. *John Hodge/DCG*

WOODHAM BROS YARD, BARRY: In the midst of the docklands of Barry there is an area of land known as West Ponds that was developed by the Dock Authority for wagon storage and marshalling purposes. When the area of sidings became redundant, the Dock Authority leased the land to Woodham Bros, railway dismantlers. During the late '50s the first batches of condemned locomotives arrived to await their fate as British Railways began the irrevocable transition from steam to diesel and electric power. The inflow of redundant steam locomotives continued unabated with the last consignment arriving in 1967, being an assortment of BR Standard classes. The number of locomotives and variety of designs represented was considerable and the yard soon became a mecca for preservationists who were looking for suitable candidates for restoration. In 1968 ex-Midland '4F' 0-6-0 No 43924 became the first of over 200 locomotives to win a reprieve from the cutter's torch.

When visited on 2 June 1978 the yard was still well stocked with a variety of rusty hulks decaying in the salty air blowing in from the Bristol Channel.

On 9 November 1989 the last locomotive, ex-GWR '2800' Class No 3845, left for the Brighton Railway Museum, and this unique chapter in steam locomotive history came to an end. The tracks were lifted in the summer of 1990 and the site had been cleared for re-development when re-visited in April 1994. *Both GPD*

114

BARRY PIER was opened in June 1899 when the Barry Railway extended the Island branch through a 280-yard tunnel. The new station was for use by trains operated in connection with pleasure steamers on the Bristol Channel, and was never used by regular passenger services. Prior to the re-building and provision of extended facilities at Barry Island station, excursion stock was often run through to the Pier station to enable the locomotive to run round before returning towards Barry. On 17 September 1966 a six-car DMU formation stands at the single platform in use at that time.

Decreasing use saw the closure of the Barry Pier station after the last train ran on 18 October 1971. Our April 1994 photograph, taken with the kind permission of the Barry Yacht Club, shows the location somewhat transformed. On the right, at the end of the section of fencing, the remains of an equipment cabinet can be seen; this was also visible beneath the canopy of the station building in the 1966 illustration. *John Edgington/GPD*

Vale of Glamorgan line

BARRY JUNCTION: The Vale of Glamorgan (VOG) Railway was promoted by the coal-owners of the Llynvi, Ogmore and Garw valleys to the north of Bridgend to provide a better outlet for their shipment coal than was offered by the limited facilities at Porthcawl. The line from Barry Junction opened for traffic on 1 December 1897. Pictured coming off the VOG route and passing Barry Junction signal box on 4 May 1958 with the diverted 6.46 am Fishguard Harbour to London Paddington train is 'Castle' Class 4-6-0 No 5051 *Earl Bathurst*.

The VOG continues to act as a diversionary route for weekend engineering works, and on Sunday 30 April 1995 'Express' unit No 158 819 approaches Barry with the 1018 Carmarthen to Birmingham New Street. Although Barry Junction signal box has not survived the passage of time, 'Castle' No 5051 has fared better, having been purchased for preservation in 1969 and now based at the Great Western Society's Didcot railway centre. *John Hodge/GPD*

RHOOSE: Lime and cement works at Aberthaw and Rhoose provided the only industry on the VOG line. The latter works can be seen on the right of our 4 May 1958 view of Landore (87E)-based 'Castle' Class No 5013 *Abergavenny Castle* passing through Rhoose with a diverted service for West Wales.

The corresponding view some 30 years after the withdrawal of local passenger services shows little trace of the former station, the level crossing being controlled from Aberthaw signal box. A diverted Swansea to London Paddington HST breezes through *en route* to Cardiff. *John Hodge/B. Cole*

ABERTHAW: Having called at Aberthaw station, BR Standard Class '3' 2-6-2T No 82040 sets off *en route* to Bridgend with an afternoon service on 29 September 1959. These Swindon-built locomotives were introduced in 1952-3 and a number were based at Barry during the mid-'50s. Their working life was relatively short, as many of the local or branch-line duties for which they were intended had been dispensed with by the early '60s, either through line closures or the introduction of DMUs.

A diverted London Paddington to Swansea HST service with power car No 43022 leading rounds the curve on Sunday 20 March 1994. The tracks on the far right lead down from the Aberthaw reception sidings to the Power Station, the spur in the foreground providing a link to the main line for westbound empty coal trains. *John Hodge/GPD*

LLANTWIT MAJOR had up and down through running lines in addition to the platform roads, a feature of the VOG common to both Aberthaw and Southerndown Road stations. DMUs had displaced steam on the local services in the late '50s, and on 28 March 1964 the 2.55 pm Barry to Bridgend is formed of the customary three-car unit. At that time weekday services ran throughout between Barry and Bridgend, while on Sundays there was a limited service between Llantwit Major and Barry, with certain services operating through to or from Cardiff.

Final closure of Llantwit Major came when the goods handling facilities were withdrawn in July 1967. Our view of the overgrown site in January 1994 shows a formation of Class 158 'Express' units heading towards West Wales. *Hugh Ballantyne/B. Cole*

COWBRIDGE ROAD JUNCTION to the south-east of Bridgend was where the Vale of Glamorgan line divided to either join the South Wales Main Line to the east of Bridgend station, or climb via an embankment to cross the main line and continue to Coity Junction and connect with the Llynvi and Ogmore Vale lines. On 23 November 1957 BR Standard tank No 82003 drifts down towards Bridgend with a local service from Barry. The embankment that carried the avoiding line is visible in the background.

Since the withdrawal of regular passenger services from 15 June 1964, the VOG route has been retained mainly as an alternative freight route, principally for coal traffic serving the Power Station at Aberthaw. The line is also used as a diversionary route, particularly at weekends during the winter months, when engineering work is being undertaken on the main line. An empty stock working comprising units 150 275 and 153 373 passes *en route* from West Wales to Cardiff on Sunday 26 March 1994. *John Hodge/DCG*

Cardiff stations

CARDIFF CENTRAL (1): This grandstand view from the Central Hotel was taken on 12 July 1952 and shows 'Castle' Class 4-6-0 No 5020 *Trematon Castle* departing at 10.15 with the up 'Red Dragon' service from Carmarthen to London Paddington. This prestige London service will take 3 hrs 10 mins to cover the 145 miles. On the right of the picture, ex-GWR 'Hall' Class 4-6-0 No 6909 *Frewin Hall* awaits departure with an inter-regional working to Portsmouth Harbour.

The 1995 passenger timetable reveals that the 'Red Dragon Pullman' is now operated by InterCity Great Western. The early morning departure from Swansea gives an 0725 timing from Cardiff Central, aimed at the business traveller to provide a 0915 arrival in London. The journey time for the HST formation from Cardiff to Paddington is a mere 1 hr 50 mins. On Saturday 15 April 1995 the 0932 HST from Swansea with power car 43149 leading sets off from Cardiff at 1025; this particular service will take a more sedate 2 hrs 5 mins to reach London. On the right a Class 158 'Express' unit awaits departure with the 1030 Regional Railways service to Portsmouth Harbour. *R. C. Riley/DCG*

CARDIFF CENTRAL (2): The eastern approach to Cardiff General is recorded in this illustration taken *circa* 1930 and showing GWR 'Castle' Class 4-6-0 No 4097 *Kenilworth Castle* arriving with the 8.55 am from London Paddington. On the left is a rake of Southern Railway carriages forming a Cardiff to Brighton service. Semaphore signals are still the order of the day and the original Cardiff East signal box is visible on the extreme right of the picture.

The major re-building undertaken in the early '30s saw the station expanded to provide additional platform facilities on the down side. The alterations shortened the platform from where our 'past' illustration was taken, and our view of 12 May 1995 could not be matched precisely. 'Sprinter' unit No 150 272 approaches with the 1340 Bargoed to Penarth. *J. Hubback, courtesy of John Hodge/GPD*

CARDIFF CENTRAL (3): This conversation piece was recorded at the bay platform at the west end of Cardiff General on Good Friday, 20 April 1962, where 0-6-0 Pannier tank No 9790 stands at the head of a single passenger coach and several vans. On the right a Swindon 'Cross-Country' DMU has just arrived with 1T23, the 9.35 am from Birmingham Snow Hill.

The gap in the station canopy still traces the extent of the former bay platform road, although the intervening years have seen the bay in-filled to provide wider platform accommodation and sufficient space for a flower bed. On 12 May 1995 HST power car 43147 has just arrived with the 1046 London Waterloo to Cardiff. *Michael Mensing/GPD*

CARDIFF CENTRAL (4): Our view of the main up platform at Cardiff General on Friday 8 September 1961 shows the 'Blue Pullman' in original livery on a crew training run in preparation for the introduction of this new diesel service to replace the steam-hauled 'South Wales Pullman' on the following Monday. The unit had body-side and end panels painted in medium blue, with an ivory-coloured surround applied to the windows and a grey roof. A streamlined re-design of the Pullman coat-of-arms was applied to the cab front. Passengers paid a supplementary fare to travel in these air-conditioned units, which had a diesel-electric power car at each end and auxiliary engines to supply the power for the air-conditioning.

By the time of the withdrawal of the Pullman units in the early '70s, the High Speed Train units were under development and the Western Region timetable of October 1976 saw their introduction into revenue-earning service. The HSTs now provide the staple train units for all InterCity Great Western and Cross Country services along the South Wales Main Line. On 12 May 1995 power car 43144 is at the trailing end of the 1232 Swansea to London Paddington service. *Hugh Ballantyne/GPD*

CARDIFF CENTRAL (5): On 8 June 1953 the inaugural run of a new addition to the titled trains operating between London and South Wales took place. The up 'Pembroke Coast Express' left Pembroke Dock at 7.45 am and called at Swansea at 10.35, with the arrival at Cardiff General behind 4-6-0 No 5082 *Swordfish* being recorded just prior to midday. With a stop at Newport, the train was scheduled to arrive at Paddington at 3.10 pm. As with all of the Western Region named trains of this era, chocolate-and-cream-liveried coaches were the norm.

The western approach to Cardiff's principal station has remained fairly featureless over the decades. However, the demolition of the ornate corner hotel premises visible in the 1953 illustration has left a gap in the architectural background, as our view of 12 May 1995 demonstrates. The 'Express Sprinter' unit is approaching platform 1 and will depart at 1345 with the Regional Railways South Wales and Western Cross-Country service to Liverpool Lime Street. *A. Jarvis/GPD*

CARDIFF CLARENCE ROAD: Opened as branch by the GWR in 1882 to serve the warehouses and wharves on the Glamorgan Canal, passenger services were introduced in 1894. Both the Barry and Taff Vale railways ran services to the terminus and, following the Grouping, the GWR continued the pattern of operation between either Barry Island or Penarth. A push-pull-fitted Pannier tank and stock was sufficient for traffic requirements in the early years after nationalisation, and in the final years before closure a single-car diesel unit was provided. A week prior to the withdrawal of passenger services on 14 March 1964, a railcar awaits its departure time with a Penarth working.

Our visit to the Dumballs Road Industrial Estate in April 1995 confirmed that many of the surrounding buildings are still in situ, although several, including the former Globe Hotel (the building with the spire), were in a poor and neglected state. Note the curve in the wall that follows the former alignment of the platform edge. *E. T. Gill/DCG*

CARDIFF RIVERSIDE: When opened in 1893 for the use of Barry Railway trains, Cardiff Riverside Junction was operated as a separate station. With the extension of services to and from Clarence Road in the following year, the Taff Vale also used the station for its Penarth services. Major alterations in 1932/3 saw the Riverside platforms replaced by a single island platform, which in 1940 was incorporated into Cardiff General station to form platforms 8 and 9. On 20 April 1959 '6400' Class 0-6-0PT No 6438 is about to propel its train down to Clarence Road on the final leg of its journey with the 7.46 morning service from Pontypridd.

Following the withdrawal of passenger services in 1964, the Riverside platforms were sometimes used for rugby football specials from West Wales and subsequently, until 1992, for parcels traffic. The fate of the former Riverside platforms was eventually sealed when work commenced on a £1.8 million redevelopment scheme at Cardiff Central station. In November 1993 demolition work was undertaken that was to see the site cleared and the adjoining railway embankment removed in preparation for improved access from the Penarth Road side of the station and the provision of additional car parking. In April 1995 no trace of the former platforms remained. *R. O. Tuck/DCG*

The South Wales Main Line -
Cardiff to Llantrisant

CARDIFF CANTON MPD (1): The GWR built its principal motive power depot in Cardiff adjacent to the main line just to the west of Cardiff General station. It opened in 1882 and accommodation was increased with the addition of a turntable shed in 1897. At nationalisation the allocation comprised 122 locomotives, a good proportion of which were representatives of the 'Castle', 'Hall' and 'Grange' Classes. Our view of the depot on 13 September 1953 shows examples of the latter two Classes awaiting their next turn of duty. On the right is the original straight six-road depot building, while to the left and set further back is the east face of the later turntable shed.

Closed as a steam depot in September 1962, the facilities were converted over the winter months to handle the repair and maintenance of diesel locomotives. Our view of the depot site in May 1995 shows the main shed building on the left, while the former steam depot building on the right is now used as a servicing shed. The steel-framed footbridge has been cut back to cross only the main running lines. *W. Potter/DCG*

CARDIFF CANTON MPD (2): The original coal stage at Canton was sited in front of the main shed building. When the GWR undertook work in 1931 to improve operational facilities at the depot, a new coal stage was constructed to the south of the shed buildings, and the old coal stage was abandoned although retained to support the water tank that formed the roof of the west portion of the structure. The old coal stage is visible in this view taken on 24 June 1956 of '4200' Class No 4203 of Newport Ebbw Junction (86A) passing on a down freight.

The portion supporting the water tank has survived the transition to diesel motive power and is seen in our corresponding view of 12 May 1995, with the 1300 London Paddington to Swansea HST passing on the main line. *R. J. Buckley/GPD*

CARDIFF CANTON (1): On 4 September 1960 ex-GWR 'Castle' Class 4-6-0 No 5039 *Rhuddlan Castle* provides a flurry of steam as it gathers speed following its stop at Cardiff General with a Paddington to Carmarthen working.

Our 1993 view of the location shows a brace of Class 37/7 locomotives, Nos 37676 and 37682, with a return working of empty bogie tank wagons from the Colnbrook Elf Oil Sidings heading for Waterston Sidings in West Wales. Pairs of Class 37s were once a common sight on South Wales oil trains, but Class 60s have now taken over the majority of such workings. *A. F. Smith, Peter Rowe (Printers)/GPD*

CARDIFF CANTON (2): An assortment of wagons make up the consist of the lengthy goods train seen opposite Canton Sidings Signal Box in 1960. Engine No 4213 was one of the batch of locomotives built at Swindon in 1912 to a Churchward design, the prototype of which had been built two years earlier. In all, 205 of these 2-8-0T mineral tank engines were built, primarily to cater for the short-haul requirements associated with the South Wales mineral traffic.

The 100 Class 60 Type 5 locomotives were built at the Brush Electrical Machines Works at Loughborough and were designed to satisfy BR's trainload freight requirements through into the 21st century. They first entered revenue-earning service in 1990 and have since established themselves as the staple motive power for the majority of the heavier freight trains to be seen operating along the South Wales Main Line. Block train workings don't come any heavier than the Port Talbot to Llanwern iron ore workings, and a typical train of loaded British Steel bogie hopper wagons is seen passing Canton behind No 60036 *Sgurr Na Ciche* (named after a Scottish mountain in the West Highlands) on Monday 30 May 1994. *John Hodge/DCG*

ELY (MAIN LINE): On 7 April 1953 ex-GWR 'Castle' Class No 7012 *Barry Castle* hustles through Ely (Main Line) station with an up passenger working. For many years the station was served by stopping trains operating between Cardiff and Swansea, but these services ceased in April 1959, leaving only the Cardiff to Pontypridd auto-trains to call.

Closure of Ely came in September 1962 and, with the demolition of the station, only the former station master's house was to survive to remind future generations of the station's existence. On 30 May 1994 Class 56 No 56114 *Maltby Colliery* passes the site with a consignment of imported coal being delivered from Port Talbot to British Steel, Llanwern. The former station house is visible on the right of our more elevated view from the road overbridge. *A. Jarvis/DCG*

ST FAGANS: Framed by the station footbridge, '6400' Class Pannier tank No 6411 stands on the up line with the 1.39 pm auto-train from Pontypridd to Cardiff Clarence Road. Note the GWR cast base sections of the platform bench seat, the gas lamps and the enamel 'Virol' advertisement in this 1954 view. The shuttle services between Cardiff and Pontypridd, operated as part of Abercynon's duty 'JB', were known locally as 'The St Fagans Pullman'.

St Fagans was unstaffed from 6 April 1959 and survived only until September 1962, when the Pontypridd service was withdrawn. No trace of the station remains as our view of the site on 15 April 1995 confirms. 'Express Sprinter' unit No 158 840 provides the '90s version of a two-coach train. *A. Jarvis/GPD*

ST FAGANS JUNCTION: This view down the main line from St Fagans station in 1954 shows the signals that controlled the approach to St Fagans Junction, together with the level crossing and signal box. In the distance the 12.45 auto-train from Cardiff Clarence Road to Pontypridd is heading away on to the spur that climbs up to Tynycaeau Junction on the former Barry Railway main line. The train will then continue via Creigiau, Efail Isaf, Tonteg and Treforest before arriving at Pontypridd shortly before 1.30 pm.

The line linking Tynycaeau and St Fagans junctions closed on 10 September 1962, and the view at St Fagans on 15 April 1995 shows the Portacabin now provided for the crossing keeper. Power car No 43177 heads the 1232 Swansea to London Paddington InterCity Great Western service. *A. Jarvis/GPD*

ST FAGANS VIADUCT carried the Barry Railway main line over the GWR South Wales Main Line to the west of St Fagans, and provides an appropriate frame for this delightful view of '4200' Class 2-8-0T No 5218 hurrying along the main line with a down freight on 23 March 1953.

Following the closure of the former Barry line, the track alignment was used to construct a new road link up to the M4 motorway, and as a consequence the old masonry structure was demolished in October 1981 and replaced by a modern concrete and brick overbridge. Our April 1994 illustration shows HST power car No 43010 heading the 1100 London Paddington to Swansea InterCity service. *A. Jarvis/B. Cole*

LLANTRISANT station, situated in the village of Pontyclun, was formerly the junction station that served three branches to Pontypridd, Cowbridge and Penygraig. An SLS special comprising a brace of former TVR auto-trailers visited Llantrisant on 12 July 1952, and 0-6-0PT No 6423 was recorded taking water at the end of the former Cowbridge branch bay platform. The Ely branch bay was on up side of the main line and can be seen behind the locomotive.

The station closed in November 1964 following the withdrawal of local services and the station was subsequently demolished. However, a new station named Pontyclun was opened in September 1992, built in connection with the extension of the Valley Lines services to include the Llynvi Valley route to Maesteg. The new facilities include twin platforms with block-paved surfaces, waiting shelters and ramp access for disabled passengers. On Tuesday 4 May 1993 'Sprinter' unit No 150 244 arrives with the 1322 Maesteg to Cardiff Central service. *R. C. Riley/DCG*

The Cowbridge and Ely branches

COWBRIDGE (1): Before continuing along the South Wales Main Line we will deal with two of the branch-line services operated to and from Llantrisant. The Cowbridge Railway opened its branch from Llantrisant in 1865, and Eastgate Street was the original terminus of the line, being close to the centre of this small market town set in the heart of the Vale of Glamorgan. Our 1950s view of the original station site shows the train shed still in situ to the left of the Pannier tank locomotive. Goods facilities south of Llanharry were withdrawn at the end of January 1965. However, the quarry at Llanharry continued to supply iron ore to the East Moors Steel Works at Cardiff until 1975, after which the final section of the branch was closed.

Cowbridge goods yard and buildings were eventually cleared to provide land for re-development, and our view of May 1995 confirms the total transformation of the former railway site. *Rev R. W. A. Jones/GPD*

COWBRIDGE (2): The Cowbridge & Aberthaw Railway opened its single-line extension from Cowbridge to Aberthaw on the coast on 10 October 1892, at which time the original Cowbridge station was abandoned and the replacement facilities opened on the new extension. The line to Aberthaw did not survive to pass into British Railways' ownership, having closed to passengers as early as May 1930 and to goods traffic in November 1932. The British Railways timetable of 1951 stated that there was limited accommodation provided on services between Llantrisant and Cowbridge. Our illustration of Cowbridge station on 2 May of that year shows the regular branch train unit of the period, AEC railcar No 18. The railcar was based at Llantrisant MPD, and on weekdays only would normally make ten return trips along the branch, with an additional late evening working on Saturdays. Eighteen minutes was sufficient for the journey of less than 6 miles, with three intermediate stops.

Passenger services were withdrawn from 26 November 1951, and following the removal of the track the building saw further use as the local headquarters of the British Legion prior to demolition. The May 1995 view of the location shows the extent of the housing development that has taken place in the intervening years. *R. C. Riley/DCG*

TONYREFAIL: The Ely Valley branch was opened as a mineral line by the Ely Valley Railway in 1862 as far as Penygraig, and was extended to Clydach Vale in August 1878. Passenger services between Llantrisant and Penygraig were introduced on 1 May 1901. Tonyrefail was originally the only intermediate station on the double-track branch, the other at Coed Ely being added in 1925 to serve the local mining village. Our late '50s illustration shows '1400' Class 0-4-2T No 1471, in lined green livery, standing at Tonyrefail with the auto-train for Penygraig. The combination of locomotive and single 3rd Class-only auto-trailer would make eight return trips over the branch on weekdays only, with an additional late evening working on Saturdays.

Our corresponding view of the location in May 1995 shows 'passenger traffic' of the '90s era in the Ely Valley. The houses in the background provide a physical link between the two pictures. *John Hodge/DCG*

PENYGRAIG Signal Box, the regular branch combination of locomotive No 1471 and auto-trailer, together with examples of the fashion of the mid-1950s provided the basis for this delightful portrait of a Welsh branch-line station in the steam era. Even the gas lamps on the footbridge at Penygraig station were still in use until the withdrawal of passenger services on 9 June 1958.

Goods services over the branch were withdrawn in October 1964, but the mineral line to Blaenclydach some 2 miles north of Penygraig remained open for coal traffic until April 1967. The southern section of the line between Llantrisant and Coed Ely Colliery was worked as a siding until the coking plant ended production in 1983, when the line north of Mwyndy Junction was closed. By the end of the '80s the trackbed had been cleared to enable construction of the Mid-Rhondda Bypass. *John Hodge/GPD*

The South Wales Main Line - Bridgend to Pyle

BRIDGEND (1): Returning to the main line, we reach Bridgend. Our mid-'30s view of the eastern approach to the station shows GWR 'Castle' Class 4-6-0 No 5014 *Goodrich Castle* arriving with a down passenger service for West Wales. The standard GWR Bridgend East Box and the wagon repair yard contribute to a vintage railway scene of the pre-war era.

The inevitable multi-storey car park and supermarket occupy the background of our view of the location on Monday 24 April 1995. The brace of Class 37/7 locomotives, Nos 37887 *Caerphilly Castle* and 37802, has just come off the VOG route from Aberthaw with 6C06, the 0830 MGR empties for Cwmgwrach, the coal washery and disposal point situated in the Vale of Neath. *J. Hubback, courtesy of John Hodge/DCG*

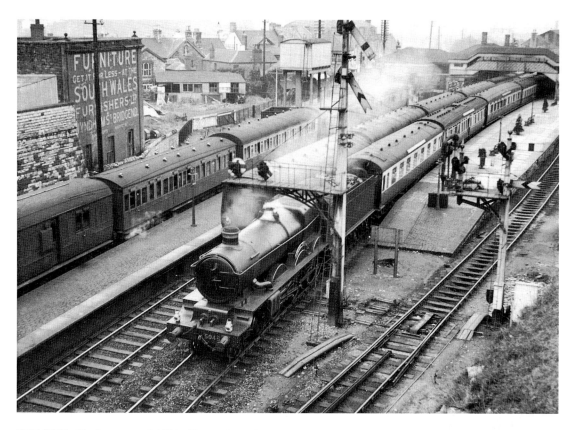

BRIDGEND (2): Our second 1930s illustration takes an overview of the east end of Bridgend station. 'Castle' Class No 5046 *Earl Cawdor* is setting off with an up passenger service for London Paddington, while on the left a train of assorted stock is waiting in the VOG bay platform. The outer face of the up platform was used by local services to and from the Mid-Glamorgan Valleys.

Class 158 'Express' unit No 158 815 arrives at Bridgend on 24 April 1995 with the Mondays-only 0841 Cardiff Central to Swansea service. With the trees on the right so well established, this view will soon be somewhat obscured by the fresh growth of leaves. *J. Hubback, courtesy of John Hodge/DCG*

STORMY DOWN: Both the train and the banking locomotive are working hard as they tackled the 1 in 93 climb from Pyle to Stormy Sidings on 14 March 1962. The train locomotive is a '4200' Class 2-8-0 tank and the banking engine an 0-6-0 Pannier tank. In steam days a Pannier tank was normally on duty at Margam Moors ready to assist eastbound freight and mineral trains.

No banking assistance was required on 24 March 1994 when Class 60 No 60036 *Sgurr Na Ciche* headed for Llanwern with a trainload of steel slab from Margam. *R. O. Tuck/DCG*

PYLE (1): The Llynvi Valley Railway Company introduced passenger services to Porthcawl in August 1865, and its station at Pyle was sited close to the GWR station on the South Wales Main Line. A junction between the main line and the Porthcawl branch was established in November 1876 and our view of the East Junction in July 1963 shows the interchange between the Cardiff and Porthcawl lines as well as the Tondu to Swansea lines. Passengers have just alighted from the 1238 service from Porthcawl and are gathering on the up main line platform to await a Cardiff-bound service. The auto-train is visible heading off into the distance for Tondu, via Cefn Junction.

Pyle station closed in 1964 and the platforms were soon demolished. There is no visible trace of the former station in our view of a passing HST bound for Swansea on Monday 29 May 1995. *D. Mathew/DCG*

PYLE (2): Ex-GWR Churchward '4400' Class 2-6-2T No 4406 stands at Pyle station on 13 September 1952 with a local working to Tondu. The locomotive was one of only ten production engines built at the Stafford Road Factory, Wolverhampton, in 1905-6, the prototype having been built at Swindon in 1904. The locomotives were intended primarily for branch-line work where route restrictions prohibited the use of heavier engines. The majority of the Class had long associations with Cornish branch lines, but 4406 and sister locomotive 4408 were allocated to Tondu for use on the Porthcawl branch. All 11 of the Class survived into British Railways' ownership, but withdrawals commenced in 1949. No 4408 was withdrawn in 1953 and 4406 was one of the final trio to be withdrawn in 1955.

The Porthcawl platforms remained in situ following track recovery, but our May 1995 visit to the site revealed only the brickwork of the former platform edge to be visible amongst the undergrowth.
R. J. Buckley/GPD

147

Mid Glamorgan branch lines

PORTHCAWL (1): A horse-worked tramroad was opened in 1829 to convey coal from the Llynvi Valley to the small harbour at Porthcawl. Conversion to a broad gauge railway was completed by the Llynvi Valley Railway Company by February 1864, when passenger services were introduced. With the development of more substantial dock facilities at Barry and Port Talbot, activity at Porthcawl declined, and by 1915 the inner basin had been filled in. A new passenger station was built on the reclaimed land, and during the following decades Porthcawl developed as a resort town. Our view overlooking the station site on 29 July 1955 shows ex-GWR '9400' Class 0-6-0PT No 8466 awaiting departure for Pyle.

Some 40 years later a road now occupies the former track alignment. In the centre background the single-storey building still serves as the headquarters of the Porthcawl Sea Cadets, founded in 1942. *Ian L. Wright/GPD*

PORTHCAWL (2): On a summer Saturday in July 1963, auto-fitted '6400' Class 0-6-0PT No 6419 waits to depart at 1225 for Pyle and Tondu. Scheduled branch passenger services used the main platform and the large island platform on which the photographer is standing was available for excursion traffic. The journey of just under 4 miles to Pyle would be covered in approximately 13 minutes with one intermediate stop at Nottage. Passenger services were withdrawn from 9 September 1963 and the branch was closed completely from 1 February 1965.

The May 1995 view provides no clue as to the land's use prior to the construction of the road. The traffic island displayed on the distant road sign was once the site of a level crossing, where a footbridge adjacent to the signal box provided an ideal vantage point to photograph arrivals and departures, as well as empty stock movements to and from the fan of storage sidings. *D. Mathew/GPD*

GILFACH GOCH: The Ely Valley Extension Railway completed the line from Gellirhiad Junction on the Ely Valley Railway to Gilfach Goch in 1864. Passenger services were operated from Tondu via Blackmill with the train reversing at Hendreforgan to complete the final leg of the journey to this small mining community. Withdrawal of passenger services came as early as September 1930, but workmen's trains continued to operate to a platform adjacent to Britannia Colliery half a mile north of the former passenger station. On 13 July 1957 an SLS special was run for enthusiasts, and our view looking north from the colliers' platform shows the train engine, ex-GWR 2-6-2T No 5574.

Closure of the branch came in June 1961 and by the time of our visit to the location in May 1995, considerable work had been undertaken to clear the mounds of colliery spoil that once dominated the landscape. *Ian L. Wright/GPD*

MAESTEG CASTLE STREET: The Llynvi Valley Railway Company had introduced passenger services between Bridgend and Maesteg in February 1864. On 15 October 1960 our photographer has caught the eye of the crew of '5700' Class Pannier tank No 9609, which is working the afternoon Bridgend to Blaengwynfi service. The British Railways timetable for the period listed nine return workings on weekdays only between Bridgend and Cymmer Afan, with the majority continuing on to serve Blaengwynfi. Passenger services were withdrawn from 22 June 1970 and the daily funded school service from Cymmer ceased soon afterwards, with Castle Street station closing in July.

Fortunately, the Llynvi Valley line remained in use for coal traffic with the remaining workings clearing surface stocks from the site of the former St Johns Washery to the north of Maesteg. On 30 September 1992 the line to Maesteg was re-opened to provide a new hourly passenger service to and from Cardiff via Bridgend. The former Castle Street station site remained derelict, however, as the new Maesteg station was sited approximately 200 metres down the line, being closer to the town centre. The last of the Llynvi coal was cleared from the site by a train on 23 February 1993 and our view of the Castle Street site in April 1995 shows the rusty track still in situ. *E. T. Gill/DCG*

TONDU: The Llynvi Valley Railway Company introduced passenger services from Tondu to Porthcawl in August 1865. Our April 1952 view of Tondu Junction records Class '4500' 2-6-2T No 4557 with a two-coach train of suburban stock that had just arrived from Pyle.

The withdrawal of passenger services from the various valley lines that radiated from Tondu was to leave only the coal traffic to provide operational activity at this once busy junction, the former station being cleared of buildings and the platforms left derelict. On Tuesday 4 May 1993 Class 37/7 No 37895 eases its train of MEA coal wagons forward as it approaches Tondu signal box to take the line up the Garw Valley with 6B65, the 0820 Swansea Burrows Sidings to Pontycymmer. Just visible on the left is the car park that was provided when the adjacent Bridgend platform at Tondu was reopened for passenger services on the Maesteg line in the previous autumn. *Ian L. Wright/DCG*

BRYNMENYN JUNCTION station was set in the junction fork where the Garw and Ogmore Vale branches divided. On 3 May 1958 '9400' Class 0-6-0PT No 8497 was photographed arriving at the Ogmore Vale up platform with the 3.50 pm Bridgend to Nantymoel service.

The former station site was considerably overgrown when visited in April 1994 to record the return working of Class 37/7 No 37896 with the 7C65 Pontycymmer to Jersey Marine Steel Supply. This reclamation scheme commenced in November 1991 and has seen large tonnages of coal removed from the tips at the head of the Garw Valley by rail. *R. O. Tuck/DCG*

BLAENGARW: The GWR opened the branch from Brynmenyn Junction to Blaengarw on 25 October 1876. During the short period of British Railways ownership the services comprised only a handful of return workings to Brynmenyn, where connections to and from Bridgend were made via the Ogmore Vale services. On 2 August 1951 Pannier tank No 9660 waits at Blaengarw with the customary pair of vintage ex-GWR coaches. The line continued beyond the station to serve Garw Colliery and Washery.

Passenger services were withdrawn on 9 February 1953 although the line remained open for the mineral traffic generated by the colliery until 1985. The former station site at Blaengarw was visited in April 1993 and by then had been cleared of all railway infrastructure. However, only a mile down the valley is the rail-served loading pad at Pontycymmer, from where trains have been clearing coal stocks extracted from the former colliery tips. *R. C. Riley/DCG*

BLACKMILL: On the final day of passenger services on 3 May 1958, auto-fitted Prairie tank No 5524 sets off from Blackmill station with the 2.55 pm return working from Nantymoel to Bridgend. Dominating the station platform is the imposing structure of Blackmill Junction Signal Box. No 5524 was one of the 100 later examples of the '4575' Class of light tank engines based on an original Churchward design of 1906; it was built at Swindon in 1927. In 1953 it had been included in the conversion work undertaken on 15 of the '4575' series of engines that were equipped with auto apparatus to operate push-pull services in the Cardiff valleys and Bridgend area.

Following closure of the line, the former trackbed has been restored and coated with a strip of tarmac to provide a cycle path for leisure activities. A passing cyclist provided a timely demonstration of this pastime when the site was visited in August 1993. In the centre of the picture the brick base of the former signal box is clearly visible, and to the right the posts of the former station nameboard are still in situ. *R. O. Tuck/DCG*

OGMORE VALE WASHERY: On 11 March 1982 Class 37/0 No 37229 passes the Ogmore Vale Central Washery with a train of loaded MDV wagons. The locomotive will continue up the valley to beyond Caedu signal box before propelling back to cross into the Washery sidings. Sited approximately 3 miles south of Nantymoel, the Washery received trainloads of coal from collieries in the Ogmore and Garw Valleys.

Wyndham Colliery in the Ogmore Vale closed in 1983 and closure of the Ogmore Vale branch came in 1985, when coal traffic from Garw Colliery ceased. The railway infrastructure had been removed and the Washery site cleared well before our visit in May 1995. However, the allotments continue in use, albeit with alterations both to sections of the fencing and the sundry associated structures! *R. L. Masterman/GPD*

OGMORE VALE: On 3 May 1958 auto-fitted '4575' Class No 5524 arrives at Ogmore Vale with the 1.55 pm service from Bridgend to Nantymoel. The leading coach, No W171, was one of the second batch of ten bow-ended auto-trailers built in 1930 for general branch-line work. The small-inward opening hammered glass ventilators were a common feature of the three batches of trailers built by the GWR in the 1929-33 period. Several examples of this second batch saw service in the South Wales valleys and remained in service until about 1958-60, to be left redundant by either train service withdrawals or the introduction of diesel units.

Following the closure of the branch in 1985 and the recovery of the railway infrastructure, the station site was cleared of the redundant buildings and in due course a footpath and cycle way was created along the former track alignment. At the former station site a rest area with seating has been created, complete with a Distant signal, as can be seen in our view of the location in August 1993. *R. O. Tuck/GPD*

NANTYMOEL: The Ogmore Valley Railway Company opened the line from Nantymoel to join the Llynvi Valley Railway line at Tondu on 1 August 1865. A merger between the two companies then followed and in 1873 the Llynvi & Ogmore Railway was absorbed by the GWR. The Ogmore Vale branch was served by half a dozen return workings to Bridgend on weekdays only during the early '50s, with the customary late evening return working each Saturday. On the final day of passenger services, 3 May 1958, the driver of '9400' Class 0-6-0PT No 8497 has a brief chat with a passenger before taking the afternoon departure down the valley.

Visited in August 1993, the site had been totally cleared and only the flat expanse of waste ground marked the course of the former railway. *E. T. Gill/GPD*

INDEX OF LOCATIONS